Conversations with Elizabeth Bishop

Literary Conversations Series

Peggy Whitman Prenshaw
General Editor

Conversations
with Elizabeth Bishop

Edited by
George Monteiro

University Press of Mississippi
Jackson

Books by Elizabeth Bishop

North & South. Boston: Houghton Mifflin, 1946.
Poems: North & South—A Cold Spring. Boston: Houghton Mifflin, 1955.
The Diary of "Helena Morley" (translation). New York: Farrar, Straus and
    Cudahy, 1957.
Brazil (with the editors of *Life*). New York: Time Incorporated, 1962.
Questions of Travel. New York: Farrar, Straus and Giroux, 1965.
The Ballad of the Burglar of Babylon. New York: Farrar, Straus and Giroux, 1968.
The Complete Poems. New York: Farrar, Straus and Giroux, 1969.
An Anthology of Twentieth-Century Brazilian Poetry (with Emanuel Brasil).
    Middletown, CT: Wesleyan University Press, 1972.
Geography III. New York: Farrar, Straus and Giroux, 1976.
The Complete Poems 1927–1979. New York: Farrar, Straus and Giroux, 1983.
The Collected Prose. New York: Farrar, Straus and Giroux, 1984.
One Art: Letters. Edited by Robert Giroux. New York: Farrar, Straus and
    Giroux, 1994.

Copyright © 1996 by the University Press of Mississippi
All rights reserved
Manufactured in the United States of America

99   98   97   96   4   3   2   1

The paper in this book meets the guidelines for permanence and durability of the Committee
on Production Guidelines for Book Longevity of the Council on Library Resources.

Library in Congress Cataloging-in-Publication Data

Bishop, Elizabeth, 1911–1979.
    Conversations with Elizabeth Bishop / edited by George Monteiro.
        p.   cm. — (Literary conversations series)
    Includes bibliographical references and index.
    ISBN 0-87805-871-0 (alk. paper). — ISBN 0-87805-872-9 (pbk. :
alk. paper)
        1. Bishop, Elizabeth, 1911–1979—Interviews.   2. Women poets,
American—20th century—Interviews.   I. Monteiro, George.
II. Title.   III. Series.
PS3503.I785Z464   1996
811'.54—dc20   95-39349
                                                            CIP

British Library Cataloging-in-Publication data available

Contents

Introduction

A quarter century after her death Elizabeth Bishop's two closely kept personal secrets are secrets no more. It is an indication of what has happened to the public regard for privacy in our time that her biographer can present the evidence for Bishop's alcoholism and lesbianism almost as matter-of-factly as she does the details of the publication of her books. While alive, however, the poet determinedly if quietly waged a successful defense against such unwanted (and potentially destructive) exposure. A natural shyness kept the poet out of the limelight even as it served to keep public attention where it belonged—on the poems. She was preternaturally cautious about what she allowed herself to say to interviewers.

Since she was reluctant to grant interviews in the first place, it is understandable that Bishop preferred to have those interviews she did grant take place in familiar surroundings. The locus in Brazil was either the Fazenda Samambaia in Petrópolis, the Leme beach apartment in Rio, or Casa Mariana in Ouro Prêto. In Boston the interviewer was invited to her condominium apartment in a refurbished warehouse at Lewis Wharf. On visits to New York City she chose to see interviewers at her club, the Cosmopolitan. In these places she was apparently more relaxed than when she was on the road, as in Holland to attend an international art festival, in Norman, Oklahoma, to receive a prize, or in Seattle, to teach for the first time as a replacement for the late Theodore Roethke.

Toward the end of the 1977 interview conducted in Boston by the poet George Starbuck, Bishop apologized for not having said "anything profound." In her interviews "Miss Moore always said something to make one think very hard about writing, about technique," she lamented, "and Lowell always says something mysterious." Indeed, it is a hallmark of the Bishop interview that she avoided, almost studiously, any semblance of seeming profound or at all mysterious, preferring, it would seem, to allow her poems to "speak" whatever claims for profundity or mystery the poet might have allowed herself.

Elizabeth Bishop was very careful about what she said in interviews and conversations that might become the basis for journalistic pieces or feature stories. Transcripts of interviews were submitted at her insistence for approval and "correction" prior to publication. The survival among Elizabeth Bishop's papers at Vassar College, for instance, of earlier versions of the interviews granted to the poet George Starbuck and to the student reporter from Bennington College, suggest that she might have set conditions for vetting when granting interviews. Sometimes, lacking such control, as with a 1975 story in the *Chicago Tribune* based on an interview, she complained about how the interviewer had made her appear. Elizabeth Spires had asked her about her fear of being misrepresented in interviews as well as the perceived interpretation of her refusal to allow her work to be published in anthologies of women poetry as "a kind of disapproval of the feminist movement." "I've always considered myself a strong feminist," countered Bishop; "[yet] after I talked to the girl for a few minutes, I realized that she wanted to play me off as an 'old-fashioned' against Erica Jong, and Adrienne [Rich], whom I like, and other violently feminist people. Which isn't true at all." The greater problem, though, was that the interviewer got some of her ideas all wrong. "I had said that I didn't believe in propaganda in poetry. That it rarely worked," Bishop corrected. "What she had me saying was, 'Miss Bishop does not believe that poetry should convey the poet's personal philosophy.' Which made me sound like a complete dumbbell!"

As private a person as she was, however, and as cautious as she was about protecting the details of her private life, Bishop was never really averse to granting interviews. She preferred, as a matter of course, to have them conducted by friends or acquaintances whenever possible. Such "controlled" interviews were especially conducive to circumspect answers tending to emphasize the same things, to the retailing of the same central anecdotes. Hence, she insisted on telling the story that a violent allergic reaction to cashews eaten on her arrival in Brazil in 1951 caused her to miss the sailing of her ship, thus initiating her long stay in the post-lapsarian tropical paradise that was Rio de Janeiro. She does not acknowledge that this illness had enabled what Bishop might have wanted from the beginning, the flowering of her love for Lota de Macedo Soares, the Brazilian woman who became her closest companion.

In interviews she remained to the end of her life as discreet as she was in the poetry she published during her lifetime. When interviewed by *Time* magazine for a cover piece on her friend and fellow-poet Robert Lowell, she spoke out against the so-called "confessional" poetry of her contemporaries, calling it "something new in the world."[1] "I hate confessional poetry, and so many people are writing it these days," she told Wesley Wehr. "Besides, they seldom have anything interesting to 'confess' anyway. Mostly they write about a lot of things which I should think were best left unsaid." Nor did she care for the Beats, finding them to be, as she said to Tom Robbins in Seattle, both "Romantic and self-pitying." The confessional poets and the Beats were too much, as she put it to Leslie Hanscom, of "the oh-the-agony-of-it school."

Bishop's repudiation of both Beat and confessional poetry seems to have had a strong basis in her aesthetic sense of what poetry should be and do. But it also had a basis in personal character. "Can one ever have *enough* defenses?" she emphasized to Wehr. She "believed," as she said, "in closets, closets, and more closets."[2] The end of poetry was not self-expression, an idea that she found confirmed when she took up teaching. "Those students are *not* there to 'express' themselves," she told Wehr; "they're there to learn how to write a *good poem*."

Bishop seemed always ready to talk about her requirement that poetry be accurate, even if, as Robert Lowell insisted—she told David McCullough—she carried "the accuracy business too far." She had lost the three houses of "One Art" in Key West, Petrópolis, and Ouro Prêto, she told David McCullough. And "The Fish" was about a catch she made in Key West. "I always *try* to stick as much as possible to what *really* happened when I describe something in a poem," she told Wehr, though in "The Fish" she did admit to changing the number of hooks hanging from the fish's mouth from three to five because "sometimes a poem makes its own demands." Similarly, she admitted to discovering that she had conflated stories in two issues of the *National Geographic* in 1918 into the single one described in "In the Waiting Room" but decided, as she told David McCullough, not to change the poem because "it was right the way it

was." Perhaps what she really meant by accuracy, was not so much
the slavish following of descriptive details or actual incidents but a
faithful adherence to what was possible in the real world. This is the
point she wished to make when she complained—as reported by Dana
Gioia—that her students took for "reality" the Joy dishwasher soap
commercial that showed forth the reflection of a human face from the
surface of a polished dish. To her this image was impossible—"You
can never see your face in a plate"—and therefore unavailable to
the writer.

She did not much like literary critics, preferring to talk about them
rather than "criticism," just as she preferred talking about poems to
talking about poetry. "Critics find the most extraordinary philosophies that never could have occurred to you when you wrote the
poem," she complained to Eileen McMahon. To understand a poem,
she advised her students, Gioia recalls, to "use the dictionary. It's
better than the critics." But she read what was written about her by
the critics and reviewers, and often her answers to questions strike
the reader as answers to often unspecified comments on her work.
"I'm not interested in big-scale work as such," she told Ashley
Brown. "Some things needn't be large to be good." On the relative
paucity of human subjects in her poetry, she admitted to Anna
Quindlen, "I think geography comes first in my work, and then
animals. But I like people, too; I've written a few poems about
people." The question of being "very object-struck" also comes up
in the interview with Alexandra Johnson. "Critics have often written
that I write more about things than people. This isn't conscious on
my part," she explains. "I simply try to see things afresh. A certain
curiosity about the world around you is one of the most important
things in life. It's behind almost all poetry." In the same interview
she answered those critics who charged her with being "merely a
descriptive poet," countering that descriptive poetry is not "such a
bad thing at all if you've done it well." After all, "the imagination
does have its own geography." Still, there is evidence that she chafed
under the charge, for, to Edward Lucie-Smith in 1964, she said: "It's
too easy to write descriptive poetry. I want to avoid the picturesque,
to write something more abstract."

Charges about her feminism or, more commonly, what appeared to
be her un-feminist behavior were a constant nettle to her, as were the

insensitive anti-feminist attitudes taken toward her work. She was not "a flaming militant," she admitted to Eileen Farley, but she was acting as a feminist when she refused, as she did throughout her career beginning in the 1930s, to allow her work to appear in anthologies devoted to women's poetry. "You read a very favorable review of a writer, saying she is very clever and talented and you think this writer must be wonderful," she told Eileen Farley. "Then, at the end, it says 'Best book written by a woman,' and all that has gone before loses its value." "Some of the most wonderful reviews I've had have been ruined because at the end they'll say, 'This is the best book by a woman in this decade.' I've been taking that all my life," she told Joan Zyda. "I've always been more interested in visual things than politics. But I was, and am, a feminist; and that is why I refuse absolutely to contribute to all-women volumes or all-women readings," she said with finality to Sheila Hale in 1978.

In her later years Bishop became more open, perhaps less circumspect, with interviewers. When, in 1978, the editor of the *Paris Review* wanted to include her in their famous interview series, she even complained, "they should have interviewed me at the same time they interviewed everybody else."[3] And though they got her to agree that the teacher-critic Helen Vendler, a Boston acquaintance, would undertake such an interview, Bishop's death in 1979 occurred before the interview could take place. The result was that the *Paris Review* finally, in 1983, published in its series Elizabeth Spires's (augmented) piece, based on conversations with Bishop, that had appeared in the *Vassar Quarterly* in 1979.

The interviews and conversations gathered in this collection can be roughly divided into those published in English and those in other languages, five in Portuguese and one in Dutch. The non-English interviews are published in English translation for the first time. In them the questions answered and the emphases placed on certain areas of Elizabeth Bishop's experiences are somewhat different from the answers given in the English-language items. The main themes of her first Brazilian interviews are the circumstances and reasons for her decision to live in Brazil, her preferences in literature, American and Brazilian—matters more directly of interest to Brazilian readers. It is in these that Bishop lists the Brazilian poets and writers who interest her most, such as Carlos Drummond de Andrade, João Cabral de Melo Neto, Manuel Bandeira, and Vinícius de Moraes, the last-named a serious poet whose larger fame rests on his having written the lyrics to the popular song "The Girl from Ipanema." While in the interview conducted during an arts festival in Ouro Prêto, where she bought a Colonial house in 1965, she is quite naturally asked questions about the festival itself and what she would do, given the power to do so, to improve living conditions in Ouro Prêto. She would push for an extensive sewage system throughout the city, similar to the septic system she had been the first to install in Ouro Prêto. Indeed some of her Brazilian interviewers attempt to present Bishop as a social and political critic of Brazil, as does Léo Gilson Ribeiro. Even his attempt to make political capital of "The Burglar of Babylon," however, owes more to his own politics than it does to Bishop's social and political thinking about Brazil. As she revealed to Ashley Brown in 1966, well after the *coup d'etat* that had turned Brazil into a dictatorship of the military, she was opposed "to political thinking as such for writers." There is no unmistakable public criticism of the way Brazil treats its beggars, for instance, until the late poem, "Pink Dog," was published posthumously in 1979. As late as 1977, speaking to Beatriz Schiller, she reveals not only that she has no theories about Brazil but that her leaving Brazil has nothing to do with Brazilian politics. The interviews conducted in English and published in English-language journals and newspapers tend to place greater stress on Bishop's own poems and her theories about poetic practice overall. She was not always pleased with how her words came out or how her ideas were translated. "This is why one gets nervous about interviews," she complained to Elizabeth Spires.

Demands on her time, such as interviews and questionnaires, brought her stress. John Ciardi's request for a five-thousand word answer to a questionnaire to American poets at mid-century evoked from Bishop barely three hundred words of largely an attack on "the analysis of poetry," which, she warned, "is growing more and more pretentious and deadly."[4] Bishop's own talk about the sources of poetry is strangely evasive, in an interesting way. "There's nothing complicated about it; it's like making a map. Eventually all the pieces fall in place," she told Sally Ellis in 1950. "Occasionally I lose a scrap and then there's trouble. I remember once I lost a key scrap and that poem never did get written." In London, in 1964, to Edward Lucie-

Smith she insisted rather nebulously on the need to have "an open
mind, letting things happen, seizing on something random that floats
through the air." In 1966, to Ashley Brown, she repeated the notion:
"A group of words, a phrase, may find its way into my head like
something floating in the sea, and presently it attracts other things to
it." To George Starbuck, a decade later, she was as noncommital as
ever, noting that "it takes probably hundreds of things coming together at the right moment to make a poem and no one can really
separate them out, and say this did this, that did that." And what is
the one quality that every poem should have? "Surprise," she answers Alexandra Johnson's question. "The subject and the language
which conveys it should surprise you. You should be surprised at
seeing something new and strangely alive." These impressionistic
statements on the randomness of what might be called poetic inspiration (though she resisted the term) tell us something about Bishop's
rather malleable way of thinking about the poetic process, though one
might find it difficult to construct an *ars poetica* out of them. They
are of a piece, however, with her answer to Elizabeth Spires's
question, "As a young woman, did you have a sense of yourself as a
writer?" "No, it all just happens without your thinking about it," she
said. "I never meant to go to Brazil. I never meant doing any of these
things. I'm afraid everything has just *happened*."

About her reading and her predecessors among the poets she tended
to be both specific and concrete. W. H. Auden, Gerard Manley
Hopkins, T. S. Eliot, Wallace Stevens, John Donne, and George
Herbert are all early favorites, with the author of *The Temple* emerging
as perhaps the strongest influence on her work. To Sheila Hale she
repeats with approval what Coleridge said about Herbert, "that he
wrote about the most fantastic things imaginable in perfectly simple
everyday language," adding that "that is what I've always tried to
do." She traced one of the marked characteristics of her own poetry
to a treatise on seventeenth-century Baroque prose that "tried to
show that Baroque sermons (Donne's, for instance) attempted to
dramatize the mind in action rather than in repose," she told Ashley
Brown, by "the use of the present tense." "Switching tenses always
gives effects of depth, space, foreground, background, and so on."
One need only think of the last line of "One Art" to see a variation of

the principle as she changes voice to achieve a similar effect: "though it may look like (*Write* it!) like disaster."

The sources of the interviews and the pieces based on conversations with Elizabeth Bishop are varied. As might be expected, when she took on a job, as Consultant in Poetry at the Library of Congress or in teaching at the University of Washington, she seemed willing enough to talk to local newspapers. Hence we have interviews from Norman, Oklahoma, where Bishop visited late in life to accept the Neustadt Prize, and Seattle, Washington, where she taught in 1966. When in Europe at an exhibition/conference in the Netherlands she was interviewed by the Dutch writer, J. Bernlef, who also translated some of her poetry.

In Brazil, it was receiving a Pulitzer Prize for poetry that sparked the interest of Brazilian journalists in the honored American poet living in their midst. The interview in *O Globo,* published on May 12, 1956, was picked up by other Brazilian newspapers. The public attention occasioned by the Pulitzer was welcomed by Bishop and her friend Lota for it gave Bishop the poet credibility, something that Brazilians had largely denied her. It was as something of a local celebrity that the unnamed reporter for *Visão,* a São Paulo magazine, interviewed her during Ouro Prêto's spring festival in 1969. It is refreshing to hear her speak as an outsider-insider on what she would try to accomplish in Ouro Prêto, the locale of her Casa Mariana, were she in charge of the government. This interview appeared in Portuguese, as did the others conducted by Brazilians, and it is unlikely, therefore, that Bishop was able to exercise the same editorial control over it as she did over the interviews she granted to American friends and poets, such as Ashley Brown, George Starbuck, and Elizabeth Spires.

The pieces in this book are reprinted in their entirety, with the exception of the pieces published in the Brazilian journal *Visão* and the English magazine *Harpers and Queen* where material unrelated to Elizabeth Bishop has been omitted. There is some repetition since the poet tended to tell the same anecdotes about herself regarding her arrival in Brazil, her unexpected but fateful decision to stay on, and the way the ordinary people of Brazil reacted to the news that she was a prize-winning poet. This very repetition reveals something about the way Bishop was able to control those Brazilian interviewers who were not acquaintances, as Beatriz Schiller was. In newspaper interviews, paragraph breaks have been omitted. In all texts titles of books have been regularized into italics. In two instances, the omission of quotations from Bishop's poems has been indicated in footnotes.

The generosity and help of several individuals facilitated my work in the identification and gathering of the pieces in this volume. I wish to thank Carlos Daghlian, who provided copies of most of the Brazilian materials, Luiz Valente, who located the interview in *Visão*, Catherine Barel, who translated J. Bernlef's interview from Dutch into English, Carla Rickerson of the University of Washington, Nancy MacKechnie, Curator of Rare Books and Manuscripts, and her staff at Vassar College, and Elizabeth Coogan and the Interlibrary Loan staff at Brown University.

My introduction has benefited from the tactful editing of Brenda Murphy. I am grateful for her help.

I am solely responsible for the English translations of those pieces that originally appeared in Portuguese.

GM
August 1995

Notes

1. "Poets: The Second Chance," *Time* (June 2, 1967), p. 68.
2. *Remembering Elizabeth Bishop: An Oral Biography,* compiled and edited by Gary Fountain and Peter Brazeau (Amherst: University of Massachusetts Press, 1994), pp. 327, 330.
3. *Remembering Elizabeth Bishop,* p. 342.
4. Elizabeth Bishop, "It All Depends," in *Mid-Century American Poets,* ed. John Ciardi (New York: Twayne, 1950), p. 267.

Chronology

1911   Elizabeth Bishop, daughter of William Thomas Bishop and Gertrude Bulmer Bishop, is born in Worcester, Massachusetts on 8 February. In October her father dies.

1915   The poet's mother is committed to Nova Scotia Hospital.

1916–18 Lives with grandparents in Nova Scotia and Worcester, Massachusetts

1927–30 Attends Walnut Hill School, Natick, Massachusetts; writes for *The Blue Pencil,* the school's literary magazine.

1930   Enters Vassar College

1933–34 Joins in the publication of *Con Spirito,* a rival to the *Vassar Review*

1934   Meets Marianne Moore; death of the poet's mother; graduates from Vassar with a degree in English literature; moves to Greenwich Village.

1935   Visits Europe for the first time

1938   Purchases house in Key West, Florida

1942   Meets Lota de Macedo Soares in New York; visits Mexico.

1945   Receives the Houghton Mifflin Poetry Prize Fellowship

1946   Houghton Mifflin publishes *North & South*

1947   Awarded a Guggenheim Fellowship; meets Robert Lowell.

1949   Appointed Consultant in Poetry at the Library of Congress

1950   Receives an American Academy of Arts and Letters Award

1951   Receives the first Lucy Martin Donnelly Fellowship, awarded by Bryn Mawr College. Starts out on a sea voyage along the coast of South America, stopping in Brazil for a short visit, which because of illness turns into a stay lasting nearly two decades; Moves in with her friend Lota de Macedo Soares in Rio de Janeiro and Petrópolis.

1953   Receives the 1952 Shelley Memorial Award; publishes two autobiographical stories in the *New Yorker*.

1954   Elected to lifetime membership in the National Institute of Arts and Letters

1955   Houghton Mifflin publishes *Poems: North & South—A Cold Spring,* which reprints her first book, along with a new collection.

1956   Awarded the Pulitzer Prize for Poetry; receives a *Partisan Review* Fellowship; Chatto and Windus, in London, publishes *Poems*.

1957   Receives an Amy Lowell Traveling Fellowship; Farrar, Straus and Cudahy publishes *The Diary of "Helena Morley,"* Bishop's translation of Alice Brant's *Minha Vida de Menina*.

1960   Receives a Chapelbrook Foundation Award

1961   Takes trips down the Amazon and, with Aldous Huxley, Mato Grosso

1963   *Brazil,* a volume in *Life*'s "World Library," is published by Time Incorporated.

1964   Receives an Academy of American Poets Fellowship; travels to Italy and England; publishes translations of three stories by Clarice Lispector in the *Kenyon Review*.

1965   *Questions of Travel,* her third book of poems, is published by Farrar, Straus and Giroux; buys a colonial house in Ouro Prêto, which she names "Mariana."

1966   Teaches for the first time, at the University of Washington in Seattle

1967   Takes a trip down the Rio São Francisco; Chatto and Windus, in London, publishes *Selected Poems*.

1968   Receives an Ingram-Merrill Foundation Grant; Farrar, Straus and Giroux publishes *The Ballad of the Burglar of Babylon*.

1969   *The Complete Poems* is published by Farrar, Straus and
        Giroux. Receives the National Book Award and the Brazil-
        ian government's Order of Rio Branco. Smith College
        awards her an honorary degree.

1970   Teaches at Harvard University for the first time

1972   Takes trip to Ecuador, the Galapagos Islands, and Peru.
        Wesleyan University Press publishes *An Anthology of
        Twentieth-Century Brazilian Poetry,* a collection in English
        translation, co-edited by Bishop and Emanuel Brasil. Re-
        ceives honorary degrees from Rutgers University and
        Brown University.

1973   Takes trip to Sweden, Finland, Leningrad and Norway

1974   Receives the Harriet Monroe Poetry Award; buys an apart-
        ment on the Boston waterfront.

1976   Receives the *Books Abroad*/Neustadt International Prize for
        Literature; travels in Portugal. Farrar, Straus and Giroux
        publishes *Geography III*. Elected to the American Academy
        of Arts and Letters.

1977   Receives the National Book Critics Circle Award

1978   Awarded her second Guggenheim Fellowship

1979   Receives honorary degrees from Dalhousie University, Hal-
        ifax, Nova Scotia, and Princeton University; Dies on 6
        October of a cerebral aneurysm.

Conversations with Elizabeth Bishop

U.S. Poetry Chair Holder Tells
How She Courts the Muse

Sally Ellis / 1950

Reprinted from the *Boston Post Magazine,* 8 January 1950, 5.

Washington, D.C.,—There are strange goings-on up on the attic floor
of the Library of Congress!

In a 24-foot office that looks so much like a Beacon Hill drawing-
room that you expect tea and thin bread-and-butter sandwiches to be
served any minute, an attractive young woman sits at her desk piecing
scraps of paper together.

Miss Elizabeth Bishop is not, however, restoring a rare, old docu-
ment. She is merely wrestling with the Muse in her own unique way.

Quiet, self-effacing Elizabeth Bishop who was born in Worcester,
is a poet and not an ordinary one either. She is the third woman to
occupy the Chair of Poetry at the Library of Congress here.

Like most poets, she does not just sit down and write—like pulling
down a window blind. She sweats it out. A stray sentence here, a
word picked up there, a phrase that comes suddenly to her mind are
all filed neatly in her memory until she can lay her hands on a scrap
of paper.

The 38-year-old consultant in poetry saves these scraps of paper
like other people collect coins and matchbook covers. Sometimes it
will be a week or again six months before she assembles all her little
scraps on her desktop and puts them together like a jigsaw puzzle.

Then Elizabeth Bishop has a poem!

"There's nothing at all complicated about it," she explained; "it's
like making a map. Eventually, all the pieces fall in place. Occasionally I lose a scrap and then there's trouble. I remember once I lost a
key scrap and that poem never did get written."

The author of *North & South* (Houghton, Mifflin, 1946), for which
she received the first special Houghton, Mifflin Poetry Prize Fellowship in 1944, Miss Bishop is one of the most promising young poets
of today.

In her position as consultant in poetry she serves the library in an advisory capacity on the acquisition, cataloging and bibliographical work connected with its poetry collections, as expert reference service in the field, and as assistant in any special projects, such as the albums of poetry recordings.

In between all this she writes poetry and is now working on her second volume of poems which she hopes to finish soon. As an authority on poetry Miss Bishop is called on to answer all kinds of questions. About 3000 letters a year inquiring about everything from the author of "Abou Ben Adhem" to "what is an appropriate poem for Mother's Day" pour into her office.

"People want to know why they can't be poet laureate," Miss Bishop laughed, "and I have to tell them that there is no such job in the United States."

The new consultant in poetry has one of those photographic memories which is invaluable in work of this kind. Not long ago, for example, a woman called from the State Department and said someone was translating an anthology of Negro poetry into Swedish and did Miss Bishop know what switch blade was? No one else in Washington seemed to!

But certainly! And she didn't have to riffle through a lot of reference material either. She shot back with the fact that it was a jackknife with a button on the side, whereupon there was a dead silence at the other end of the line. Someone must have run for the smelling salts at the State Department! Nothing ever happens that fast in official Washington.

People ask and expect Miss Bishop and her very efficient assistant to answer such questions as "Did Mary Garden ever write a poem?" and "Did Longfellow write 'Barbara Fritchie'?"

Ladies anywhere from 60 to 80 want to know if the library can find a copy of a poem given to their grandfathers. One man wanted a list of everything Robert Browning had ever written. And another asked for the complete text of Richard Crashaw's "Hymn of the Nativity" so that he could set it to music. Last week he phoned the department again to tell them it was to be played at the Cathedral in Washington the Sunday before Christmas.

Miss Bishop is expected to be not only an authority on poetry but a linguist as well: Someone called her not long ago and said, "Hey, if I read you six lines of poetry in German will you translate it?"

"We're constantly asked for poems on love, horses, marriage, dogs and death. A letter came in from Allentown, Penn., asking us for a poem on Washington with the postscript, 'Nothing too serious, though'. A soldier walked in and wanted to know the history of the limerick two days ago."

"Did you give it to him?" we asked, completely floored at Miss Bishop's sangfroid.

"Told him it was in the *Encyclopedia Britannica,*" she grinned back, "but he didn't believe me. So I looked it up myself and gave him all the information, whereupon he left, quite happy, feeling it was all very authentic."

When the cherry blossoms bloom the Chair of Poetry hauls out its Memorial Day poems to meet the deluge of requests for something appropriate to the occasion. May 30th brings the greatest number of letters for poems, but Mother's Day is a close runner-up with the Fourth of July and Christmas keeping a neck-and-neck pace.

The army and navy are forever asking for poems written during World War II, and Senators, Miss Bishop says, usually want certain parts of poems to quote in their speeches. Once in a while the White House calls to ask for a line of a certain poem for speechmaking purposes, too.

There's a "never-say-die" spirit about consultants in poetry. Once somebody asked for a poem about Christmas Day in the workhouse and Miss Bishop's assistant spent three months looking for it.

Another search was launched for "Paul Points His Pistol at the Phesians," a poem in Negro dialect but alas, it was never found. It was no easy job but the staff did successfully ferret out a poem about New York city and tenements. They found "Morals, Manners and Miseries in a Tenement House," published by Henry Laffin, 1887 and sent it along.

Some indication of the state nagging wives have put their husbands in is evidenced by the popularity of a very old poem called "Thirty Years with a Shrew." It's three pages of verse about St. Peter letting a self-righteous, nagging woman and her genial, fat, easygoing husband into heaven. The department is always getting requests on this one.

While much of the routine work of answering these letters is taken care of by Miss Bishop's assistant, knotty problems always end up on the consultant's desk. In addition to this work Miss Bishop supervises special projects such as the albums of poetry recordings the Congressional Library makes.

"With the establishment of its Recording Laboratory in 1940, the Library of Congress began to record poetry readings of visiting poets as occasion presented," Miss Bishop explained. "So many students, teachers and lovers of poetry became interested that Fellows of the Library of Congress in American Letters decided upon a systematic program of collection.

"Under Archibald MacLeish's tenure as Librarian of Congress the collection began and we now have five albums of recordings including readings by some 20 famous contemporary poets such as Robert Frost, T. S. Eliot, Marianne Moore, Karl Shapiro, Mark Van Doren and Theodore Spencer."

Miss Bishop's most absorbing task at the moment is getting out a series of recordings of these contemporary poets. Over the weekend Robert Frost was down to the Library to make an album. "He reads so beautifully," Miss Bishop sighed.

The poets are free to choose the selections they like best. Several recordings are made and Miss Bishop chooses what she considers the best records for the final album.

Although the Library's consultant in poetry was born in Worcester, educated at Walnut Hill School in Brookline and has an aunt, Miss Florence Bishop of Commonwealth Ave., most of her adult life has been spent between New York, Paris, Morocco and Key West, Florida.

This is the first time she has been in Washington and the only thing she doesn't like about it is the heavy traffic and the music they play on the street cars. Thinks it's an infringement of personal liberty and has been driven to taking taxis to work to keep her peace of mind.

A graduate of Vassar College, 1934, she first began to write poetry during her senior year. Her work received wide recognition after the publication of a poem "The Roosters" in a special poetry number of *The New Republic*.

In 1947 she received a Guggenheim Fellowship for Creative Writing. Both her poems and prose have appeared frequently in *The New*

Yorker, The Nation, Partisan Review, Harper's Bazaar and other periodicals. Many of her poems have been recorded at Harvard, by the Victor Company as well as at the Library of Congress and are included in *A Little Treasury of Modern Poetry* (Scribner's 1946). She is also represented in *Best Short Stories of 1948*.

With a glittering background like this you might think Miss Bishop would be bouncy and pleased but she isn't. "I never have any sense of elation after I've finished," she admitted.

"All I ever can see is room for improvement. In fact I don't like anything I've written very much!"

This brilliant but modest woman has two methods of working. One is to get an idea and write a poem about it. The other is to pick up a phrase without any idea behind it and develop it. She has used both with success.

The Chair of Poetry, established in 1936, is provided for by a gift of funds from Archer M. Huntington of New York. Miss Bishop succeeded Leonie Adams. Allen Tate, Robert Penn Warren, Louise Bogan, Karl Shapiro and Robert Lowell are among the famous poets who have held the Chair of Poetry.

Miss Bishop will hold the position for a year and she retains her membership among the exclusive Fellows after the expiration of her term.

Pulitzer Prize Poet Lives in Petrópolis

O Globo / 1956

Reprinted from *O Globo* (Rio de Janeiro) (May 1956).

Petrópolis, 11 (Special to *O Globo*)—It was poetry that brought Elizabeth Bishop to that bucolic retreat of Petrópolis, within the borders of Samambaia, the splendid scenery of which provides the serenity, profundity, and sweetness that are the characteristics that she to this point expresses in her poems.

The North-American poetess, now honored with a Pulitzer Prize, possesses, despite her graying hair, a young face, in which she exhibits the amenable and timid smile of a child, and eyes whose indefinite color seems to reflect, sometimes the green of the scenery, sometimes the serene blue of the sky above. She is a native of Massachusetts, 44 years old, and someone, as she declared to us, who was inspired by literature from the moment that she learned to read when she was barely five. She is a confirmed spinster, perhaps because to no one man could she dedicate her immense affective potential. She has given it to all. She likes things simple, adores planting and gardening, and knows how to cook (including a good *feijoada*).

Some four years ago Elizabeth Bishop started out on a voyage around the Americas, but interrupted it at Brazil, where she visited with her old friend Carlota de Macedo Soares, whom she had met in the United States ten years earlier. She sensed that everything in Brazil spoke to her spirit, and her emotional affinity with the vivacious and intelligent 'Dona Lotinha' was the final argument that caused her to take up residence in this country. Her answer to our question of why she made Brazil her second homeland was plain and concise, as she knows how to be:

"Because nature here is sweet and beautiful, and the people are sweet and good."

And "flying as high as they wait"—to imitate an expression from one of her poems, she ended up in that charming highland of Samambaia, where everything blends with her love for animals (she has a "hayseed" cat, whose carriage and beauty inspire envy in all the angoras that show up, as well as a striking toucan), for flowers, and for children. As for children, she wrote a lovely poem, "Squatter's Children" (for which Lúcia Miguel Pereira suggested the Brazilian title of "Filhos de Favelados"). Published in the review *Anhambi,* it offers an eloquent example of her concern with the problems of humankind.

"Every good writer takes into account the social problems of his times," she says emphatically at some point in our interview, "and in one way or another, all good poetry reflects those problems."

Questioned about how she reacted to the *Globo*'s news that she had been awarded the "Pulitzer Prize," the poetess replied that "it was a great surprise."

And when we inquired further whether in fact she had ever expected to be the recipient of such an honor, the poetess replied: "All North-American poets *hope,* naturally, to win it, yet for me it was really a surprise."

Actually Elizabeth Bishop has already won a respectable series of prizes, fellowships, and other distinctions: the Houghton Mifflin Fellowship in Poetry, 1945; Guggenheim Fellowship, 1947; Fellow in American Letters, Library of Congress, 1949–1950; Lucy Martin Donnelly Fellowship, Bryn Mawr College, 1951; Shelley Memorial Award, 1952; Partisan Review Fellowship in Poetry, 1956. In 1954 she was elected to membership in the American Institute of Arts and Letters.

As for the beginnings of her literary career, she told us that she started writing as a child, publishing in school publications into her adolescence.

Her poems were first published in book form ten years ago under the title *North & South,* thanks to her victory over eight hundred competitors for the Houghton Mifflin Fellowship in Poetry.

Now, in 1955, the poems of *North & South* have been reissued, in combination with a new collection (*Cold Spring*), as a single volume entitled *Poems.* Next year *Poems* will be published in England.

Elizabeth Bishop belongs to no school of poetry, and she has no preferred theme. She is a poet without prejudices, one who writes poetry about places, people, animals, and things, as she took pains to point out. There is lyricism, romanticism, and realism in her work, all melded in a most individual manner of poetry-making.

The North-American poetess has just translated into English *Minha Vida de Menina* by Helena Morley (who is none other than "Senhora" Mário Brant). This translation will be published simultaneously in England and the United States. She is also translating a book on architecture, written by the Brazilian architect Enrique Mindlin.

Just as Gide preferred Victor Hugo, Elizabeth Bishop singles out Walt Whitman among contemporary poets, and from the past, Chaucer and Shakespeare, along with Euripides, Aristophanes, Virgil, Dante, and Camões. Of works in prose, she points to the Bible and D. Quixote, which Irving called "the profane Bible"; and among the moderns, Mark Twain, Hawthorne, Melville, and Henry James, as well as the Hemingway of the "short stories."

"Of the Brazilian poets that I have had the opportunity to read, I prefer Manuel Bandeira [who has translated one of her poems], Carlos Drummond de Andrade, and João Cabral de Melo Neto. Of the prose-writers I know Machado de Assis, Euclides de Cunha, Gilberto Freire, Otávio Tarquinio de Sousa, Lúcia Miguel Pereira, and Raquel de Queirós. And I hope to read many others."

Since living in this country, she has written, among other poems, "Squatter's Children" and "Manoelzinho."

Among the Brazilians who most admire the U.S. poetess is Portinari, whom Elizabeth Bishop equally admires.

"Portinari does not speak English, and Elizabeth does not speak Portuguese, yet they understand each other, because art is a universal language," spiritedly observed 'Dona Lotinha.' "And the great painter always asks, 'When is she coming to visit us again?' "

Dona Carlota de Macedo Soares, who hosts this "adopted Brazilian," is the daughter of our colleague J. E. de Macedo Soares, who edits the *Diário Carioca.*

Elizabeth Bishop declares, finally, that after four years of living in Brazil, she has no idea when she will return to the United States.

Taking her leave of *O Globo,* the author of "Lullaby" sets out for her studio. It is set off, a short distance away from the beautiful and ultra modern residence of Samambaia, in the midst of the vegetation where, undoubtedly, she manages to breathe in the atmosphere of dream and rest that she writes about in her poems.

Returning in the dark, under a light, impertinent rain that insists on making us forget that winter is nearly upon us, we are reminded once again of that which has been said about this inspired poet, known only to a limited readership, even in her native land: one who is serene, profound, discreet, sweetly subtle, fine, and spontaneous—it takes such a reader to understand Elizabeth's emotional message, one in which nothing is superfluous.

No Jokes in Portuguese

Edward Lucie-Smith / 1964

Reprinted from the London *Times*, 26 July 1964, 36.

Elizabeth Bishop is an American poet of real distinction (her selected *Poems* is published here by Chatto & Windus at 8s 6d); and she has been visiting England for the first time since before the war—soft-voiced, immaculate, unflurried: and smilingly trenchant. Perhaps understandably, the only topic on which she seems a little cautious is that of Mary McCarthy's recent novel, *The Group*. As everyone knows, *The Group* is about girls from Vassar—and Miss Bishop and Miss McCarthy are not only lifelong friends, but were in fact at Vassar together.

"Mary always manages to give me a mention on the jackets of her books," says Miss Bishop, with a slightly wondering air. At the same time she confesses that she is glad "not to be one of the characters" in this particular novel. But she remains a staunch defender of the book's basic accuracy, even to minute details—"I've eaten some of the recipes myself"—and feels that its essential humour tended to pass the reviewers by. "Mary," says Miss Bishop, "is the first woman who's made fun of sex in that way."

This last remark gives a clue to the unexpectedness of conversation with Miss Bishop, which drifts from general considerations about literature and about women poets (she feels that they "get discouraged very young") to modern American poetry in particular, which she doesn't deny is different from the poetry being written in England. In part, she puts this down to the fact that American writing has been "both stimulated and slowed down" by the academic work undertaken by most American poets. She thinks that her American colleagues have more diversity than their English counterparts, are more deliberately experimental, more intellectual in their approach. She confesses that, for her, American poetry is "more surprising." A close friend of Robert Lowell's ("we go fishing together"), and a tremendous admirer of his work, she seems rather stunned by the near-canonisation which has recently overtaken Lowell here.

12

As a poet, she feels that the essential thing is "having an open mind, letting things happen, seizing on something random that floats through the air. If you're in the right frame of mind, everything strikes you as poetry." She has lived in Brazil for the past thirteen years, and admits that the exoticism of her surroundings has made things difficult for her as a writer. "It's too easy to write descriptive poetry," she says. "I want to avoid the picturesque, to write something more abstract."

About English writers, she shows herself a trifle lukewarm. "They have a certain nonchalance and frivolity at the expense of enthusiasm. I like fanatics—people who go all out." All the same, Philip Larkin's work pleases her, because "everything he writes about is so awful." Surprisingly, her greatest admiration turns out to be William Empson, and especially his much-debated recent book of criticism, *Milton's God*. She talks of Empson's critical prose: "slightly awkward, but so characteristic. Half a sentence, and you can tell it's by Empson." The book itself she finds "sad but brilliant"—and one feels that "sad" is a term of high praise with her.

Asked about her personal sympathy with Empson's attitudes, she suddenly begins to talk of her "constant horror about the degree of civilization we've reached. We congratulate ourselves quite falsely on having come a long way when we haven't." From this, it is a paradoxically easy step to one of her great admirations among the writers of the past—Charles Darwin. She mentions his *Formation of Coral Reefs:* "If you want to read a beautiful book, read that."

And as for England itself—"They scold you a great deal," she says with a twinkle. "And I'm suffering from caffeine-withdrawal. I haven't had a cup of what I'd call coffee since I got here. All the same, it's nice not to have to tell my jokes in Portuguese. But then, I've only thought of one funny thing since I got here—that being in England is rather like going to the movies after you've read the book."

Elizabeth Bishop: The Poetess, the Cashew, and Micuçu

Léo Gilson Ribeiro / 1964

Reprinted from *Correio da Manhã* (Rio de Janeiro) (Dec. 13, 1964), p. 6.

The notice in the *New York Times* specifies that the American poetess Elizabeth Bishop, who has just received a poetry prize from the Academy of American Poets, lives in Rio de Janeiro, while the London *Sunday Times* refers to the "exotic ambience" she has chosen for her permanent residence. In reality Elizabeth Bishop lives near Petrópolis, on a farm laid out by Sérgio Bernardes. The apartment in Leme where we find her belongs to her friend, Lota de Macedo Soares, who many years ago, at New York's Museum of Modern Art, first sparked her interest in Brazil.

The poetess receives us. She is surrounded by picturesque and pretty figures of "bumba-meu-boi" that she has bought at the Providência Fair and is now packing in boxes large enough to contain them for her uphill trip. In a politer version of *The Man Who Came to Dinner,* Miss Bishop arrived in Rio 13 years ago and has remained among us to this day. "It all started when I tried a cashew, a tropical fruit that I found strange. I had a violent allergic reaction to its acidic juice. It was so bad that I missed the sailing of the ship on which I was voyaging along the length of the coast of South America. Then, the Brazilians were so charming to me that I just stayed on—to this very today," she clarifies, smilingly.

We know that her poetry has been distinguished and significantly recognized by a Pulitzer Prize, as well as by fellowships from the *Partisan Review,* the Guggenheim Foundation, and others. We ask if the voluntary separation from an English-language community has not caused her difficulties in her poetic development, surrounded as she is now by a language foreign to her. "Well, I speak a good deal of English even here in Brazil. Besides, from time to time I go back to the United States, returning to my linguistic sources, like a diver

14

coming up to the surface.'' It is clear that Elizabeth Bishop does not depend, for her inspiration, on her ambience; as she declared in London: ''It is easy to write poetry that is merely descriptive, but I want to avoid exactly that element of the 'picturesque' and prefer to write something more abstract.'' But it is obvious that some Brazilian themes do permeate her poems. Two weeks ago, the *New Yorker*—the review that publishes Salinger, Baldwin, Carson McCullers and others—brought out her beautiful ''Ballad'' about Micuçu, who died on the hill of Babilonia, a poem judged by the major living American poet, Robert Lowell (her friend for over 20 years), to be ''one of the greatest ballads in the English language,'' and a poem that, strangely, reveals much more about Brazil than does the book she wrote for the *Life* World Library. Employing certain archaic terms and of an indescribable melancholy in its majestic ''andante,'' the ballad speaks of the ''favelas'' on the ''green slopes of Rio'' that are inhabited by the poor, no longer able to return to their homes, who build nests and houses—out of nothing, out of air, houses which the slightest breeze, it would seem, might blow down—on hills called Querosene, Esqueleto, Catacumba and Babilonia. Into the poem she has introduced phrases from newspapers and something from that ''literature on a string'' from the Northeast that she so much likes. In her next book, *Questions of Travel,* this passionate traveller, who is already acquainted with three-fourths of the world, groups together a series of poems inspired by Brazil.

Elizabeth Bishop considers Robert Lowell and Marianne Moore (the latter was with her in college and is one of her best friends) the most important U.S. poets of this century. ''Even T. S. Eliot would concur in this judgment,'' she explains. ''Marianne Moore is fundamental, and not only for having published poets of great intensity, such as Hart Crane, in the *Dial,* her splendid poetry review. It is difficult to define her contribution, so decisive it appears to me, but I am certain that she is our most original poetess, the one who has brought a brilliant precision to poetic language by means of a meticulous conservatism. Her extremely personalized style is at this moment influencing the young poets of the United States. She has succeeded in introducing a great variety of poetic motives, maintaining the ancestral, 'out-of-date' virtues of American culture—such as irony, a subtle sense of humor, understatement—while keeping herself at the same time within the creative vanguard of poetry in the English language."

Hoping to make Brazilian poets better known abroad, Elizabeth Bishop a short time ago translated a series of representative Brazilian poems for a volume of Latin-American poetry to be published in March by Penguin "pocket books" in England. Among the poets she selected are Carlos Drummond de Andrade and João Cabral de Melo Neto. It is her opinion that in the United States as well as Great Britain, interest in Brazilian literature, theater, architecture, etc. has increased considerably of late. "Actually, it wouldn't take much to show an increase since ignorance of Brazilian matters has been almost absolute. But now books are being published, universities offer courses in Brazilian studies—the situation is changing." Nevertheless, George Devine, that man of the English theater, in an interview accorded the *Correio da Manhã* when he passed through Rio last year, accused Brazil of not doing enough cultural publicity, insisting that our embassies, consulates, and representatives in London could do a much better job of disseminating news of all the positive things we have to offer. Miss Bishop is much too courteous to make any such direct accusations, but she agrees that a more intense program of exchange—of students, professors, critics, and artists—would greatly enhance mutual understanding between Brazil and the United States by undoing any false "clichés" that one country might have about the other.

And what are her impressions after having lived in Brazil for such a long time? Has Brazil changed much in that time? We would like to know. "One of the things one notices immediately upon arriving in Brazil is its racial democracy. One feels, with relief, that there is no tension or conflict between the races. I believe that the grave situation in my country will be resolved pacifically, in such a way that the races will live with civility side by side. I believe that over the past 5 or 6 years the progress made in such comprehension has been greater than that made in the previous 100 years. Personally, I think the greatest American contributions to the world in the artistic sector have been made precisely through the Negro, with 'jazz' and the 'blues.' Apart from that, I adore the Brazilian way of life without pressing ('unhurried'), the way the Brazilians are humane, understanding, spirited! Has Brazil changed? In essential matters, fortunately not, I think, but there are things that irritate me, such as the rank proliferation of horrible signs mutilating the beautiful scenery of Brazil—on the Rio-Petrópolis road, for example. It is a crime, believe me! But an even greater crime is to tear down, in Rio, in Minas, in so many places, those venerable edifices of great beauty, which constitute historical and artistic treasures of past epochs. Is there no way to put a stop to such wanton destruction of this nation's heritage? I reiterate that to me it is a crime against nature, against history, even against God!'' (If she knew about it, what would Miss Bishop say about the mayor of the marvelous Salvador of Bahia who ordered the demolition of the oldest Cathedral built in Brazil to make way for an immense bus and trolley car terminal?)

In conclusion, the poetess tells us about her first contact with poetry and principally about her earliest days of childhood in New England and Nova Scotia. "In origin I am half-Canadian, half-American from New England. It's amusing. Before the American Revolution my ancestors belonged to opposing parties. My father's family sided with the English and King George III, but my mother's family were Whigs (liberals) waging lively battle against the Tories (conservatives), who did not wish to separate themselves from the British Crown. I remember a childhood spent in a small city that strictly speaking, was nothing more than a village. We lived quiet, withdrawn lives, devoted entirely to the family; my dear mother churned butter at home, and I, a child, steered the cows out to pasture. When I translated into English the *Diary of Helena Morley,* an account of the author's childhood in Diamantina, I found that there were many similarities in the world she describes and that of my own childhood. Life, in that half-time, changed a good deal,'' she reflects, as she contemplates the sun-drenched curve of Copacabana beach. Then, for an instant, her gaze fixes on the hill behind the modern buildings, in which a young bandit, a victim of social circumstances, was shot to death by the police and it is as if the melody of her ballad for Micuçu, which now rings out in the iron and steel structures of Manhattan, impregnates lightly the atmosphere of the afternoon that is ending.[1]

---

1. Ribeiro quotes the first twenty lines of "The Burglar of Babylon."

An Interview with
Elizabeth Bishop

Ashley Brown / 1966

Reprinted from *Shenandoah*, 17 (Winter 1966), 3–19.

Brazil: Elizabeth Bishop's study is a small house which lies up the hill from her home in the mountains near Petrópolis, the old imperial summer capital. The study is perched above a waterfall. One looks through the windows at a clump of bamboos which descend to a tiny swimming-pool, momentary repose in the course of the cascading water. The room is filled with books, comfortable armchairs, piles of old literary quarterlies. An exquisite *oratório* from Minas Gerais and other small miscellaneous objects stand on the bookcases. A literary visitor will notice photographs of Baudelaire, Marianne Moore, and Robert Lowell near the poet's work-table. Tobias, an elderly cat, and Suzuki, his younger Siamese companion, reluctantly move from the vicinity of the typewriter.

Interviewer: I think you have one of the handsomest settings in the world. What poet could ask for more? Do you find that a dazzling landscape like this is an incentive to write, or do you prefer to shut yourself off from visual distractions when you are working?

Miss Bishop: You will notice that the study turns its back on the view of the mountains—that's too distracting! But I have the intimate view to look at; the bamboo leaves are very close. Everybody who comes here asks about the view: is it inspiring? I think I'll put a little sign saying "Inspiration" on those bamboos! Ideally, I suppose any writer prefers a hotel room completely shut away from distractions.

Interviewer: You have been living in Brazil since about 1952, haven't you?

Miss Bishop: Yes, it was the end of November, 1951, when I came here; you remember my poem, "Arrival at Santos."

Interviewer: As far as your poetry goes, have you been able to get anything from Brazil except its appearances? I mean, can you draw on the social and literary traditions here?

Miss Bishop: Living in the way I have happened to live here, knowing Brazilians, has made a great difference. The general life I have known here has of course had an impact on me. I think I've learned a great deal. Most New York intellectuals' ideas about "underdeveloped countries" are partly mistaken, and living among people of a completely different culture has changed a lot of my old stereotyped ideas.

As for the literary milieu in Brazil, it is so remote from ours. In Rio for example, the French influence is still powerful. I find the poetry very interesting, but it hasn't much to do with contemporary poetry in English. Our poetry went off in a different direction much earlier.

Interviewer: When you say our poetry went off in a different direction, what do you mean?

Miss Bishop: What happened with Eliot and Pound as early as 1910—modernism. The Brazilians' poetry is still more formal than ours—it's farther from the demotic. It is true, of course, that they had a *modernismo* movement in 1922, led by Mario de Andrade and others. But they still don't write the way they speak. And I suppose they have still never quite escaped from romanticism. It's an interesting fact that there is no word in Portuguese for "understatement." Marianne Moore's poetry is nearly all understatement. How can they understand us? So much of the English-American tradition consists of this. They have irony, but not understatement.

By the way, I lived in Mexico for a time twenty years ago and I knew Pablo Neruda there. I think I was influenced to some extent by him (as in my "Invitation to Miss Marianne Moore"), but he is still a rather "advanced" poet, compared with other South American poets.

To summarize: I just happened to come here, and I am influenced by Brazil certainly, but I am a completely American poet, nevertheless.

Interviewer: What about the Portuguese language? Do you find that reading it and speaking it (and being surrounded by it) have increased your awareness of English?

Miss Bishop: I don't read it habitually—just newspapers and some books. After all these years, I'm like a dog: I understand everything that's said to me, but I don't speak it very well. I don't really think that my awareness of English has been increased. I felt much the same when I lived in France before the war. What I really like best is silence! Up here in Petrópolis, in the mountains, it is very quiet.

Interviewer: How would you describe Portuguese as a poetic language?

Miss Bishop: From *our* point of view, it seems cumbersome—you just can't use colloquial speech in that way. Grammatically, it is a very difficult language. Even well-educated Brazilians worry about writing their own language; they don't speak their grammar, as it were. I imagine it's easier to write free verse in Portuguese—because it gets you away from the problem. They did take to free verse very quickly here.

Interviewer: Now, if I may, I'd like to recall you to North America and your childhood. You actually spent your earliest years in Nova Scotia, didn't you? Did you live in the kind of house where people encouraged the children to read? Or did your literary interests come later?

Miss Bishop: I didn't spend all of my childhood in Nova Scotia. I lived there from 1914 to 1917 during the first World War. After that I spent long summers there till I was thirteen. Since then I've made only occasional visits. My relatives were not literary in any way. But in my aunt's house we had quite a few books, and I drew heavily on them. In some ways the little village in Canada where I lived was more cultured than the suburbs of Boston where I lived later. As for the books in our house, we had Emerson, Carlyle, all the old poets. I learned to read very early, and later I used to spend all of my allowance on books. They were all I ever wanted to buy.

Interviewer: What were some of your favorite books? Were you ever deeply impressed by something you read in those days?

Miss Bishop: I was crazy about fairy tales—Andersen, Grimm, and so on. Like Jean-Paul Sartre (as he explains it in *Les Mots*), I also read all kind of things I didn't really understand. I tried almost anything. When I was thirteen, I discovered Whitman, and that was important to me at the time. About that time I started going to summer camp and met some more sophisticated girls who already knew Emily Dickinson and H. D. and Conrad and Henry James. One of them gave me Harriet Monroe's anthology of modern poets. That was an important experience. (I had actually started reading poetry when I was eight.) I remember coming across Harriet Monroe's quotations from Hopkins, "God's Grandeur" for one. I quickly memorized these, and I thought, "I must get this man's work." In 1927 I saw the first edition of Hopkins. I also went through a Shelley phase, a Browning phase, and a brief Swinburne phase. But I missed a lot of school and my reading was sporadic.

Interviewer: Did you write anything much before you went to Vassar? I remember your saying you had some exceptionally good teachers at Walnut Hill School in Natick.

Miss Bishop: I wrote a good deal, starting at the age of eight. When I was twelve I won an American Legion prize (a five dollar gold piece) for an essay on "Americanism." This was the beginning of my career. I can't imagine what I said on *this* subject! I was on the staff of the literary magazine at school and published some poems there. I had a good Latin teacher and a good English teacher at Walnut Hill. The teaching was of a very high quality. I only studied Latin then. I didn't take up Greek till I went to Vassar. I now wish I'd studied nothing but Latin and Greek in college. In fact I consider myself badly educated. Writing Latin prose and verse is still probably the best possible exercise for a poet.

Interviewer: You were in what turned out to be a brilliant literary generation at Vassar—Mary McCarthy, Eleanor Clark, Muriel Rukeyser, besides yourself. Did your friends set a high standard of criticism even in those days?

Miss Bishop: Actually I was a close friend only with Mary. Eleanor and I were friends, too, but she left for two years, and Muriel was there for just a year. Yes, they, we, were all terribly critical then. One big event for us was a little magazine we started. Mary has recently talked about this. This is the way I remember it: The regular literary magazine was dull and old-fashioned. Mary and Eleanor and I and several others decided to start one in competition. It was to be anonymous. We used to meet in a speakeasy and drink dreadful red wine and get slightly high. (Afterwards the college physician analyzed the wine and found it contained fifty per cent alcohol, she said, but I can't believe that.) We called the magazine *Con Spirito*. We got out only three numbers, I think, but we prevailed. I published several poems and stories in *Con Spirito*. T. S. Eliot came to Vassar about this time. I was elected to interview him and I was absolutely terrified. But he was very gentle, and later he flattered us by saying he liked some of the things in our magazine.

Interviewer: In those days did you think about becoming a poet or a novelist?

Miss Bishop: I never *thought* much about it, but I believe I was only interested in being a poet.

Interviewer: You grew up in the Marxist '30's. Do you think this radical political experience was valuable for writers? Or did it blunt people's perceptions to be thinking in such exclusively political terms?

Miss Bishop: I was always opposed to political thinking as such for writers. What good writing came out of that period, really? Perhaps a few good poems; Kenneth Fearing wrote some. A great deal of it seemed to me very false. Politically I considered myself a socialist, but I disliked "social conscious" writing. I stood up for T. S. Eliot when everybody else was talking about James T. Farrell. The atmosphere in Vassar was left-wing; it was the popular thing. People were always asking me to be on a picket-line, or later to read poems to a John Reed Club. I felt that most of the college girls didn't know much about social conditions.

I was very aware of the Depression—some of my family were much affected by it. After all, anybody who went to New York and rode the Elevated could see that things were wrong. But I had lived with poor people and knew something of poverty at first-hand. About this time I took a walking-trip in Newfoundland and I saw much worse poverty there. I was all for being a socialist till I heard Norman Thomas speak; but he was *so* dull. Then I tried anarchism, briefly. I'm much more interested in social problems and politics now than I was in the '30's.

Interviewer: What poets did you meet when you started moving around in the world? I believe you have known Marianne Moore for many years.

Miss Bishop: I met Marianne Moore in 1934, the last year I was in college, through Fanny Borden, the college librarian, an old friend of the Moore family. (I had read a few of her poems in anthologies.) I asked Miss Borden why she didn't have *Observations* in the college library, and she said, "Are you interested in Marianne Moore? I've known her since she was a child!" And she introduced me to her shortly afterwards.

When I was a junior, *Hound and Horn* had a contest for students. I sent in a story and a poem and got honorable mention for both. I also had a story and a poem in a magazine called *The Magazine,* run by

Howard Baker and his wife. Baker's friend Yvor Winters wrote me; I
think he wanted to take me under his wing. But nothing came of that.
He introduced me to a former student of his, Don Stanford, who was
then at Harvard.

Interviewer: Were you in any way affected by Auden during the
'30's?

Miss Bishop: Oh, yes! I started reading him in college. I bought all
his books as they came out and read them a great deal. But he didn't
affect my poetic practice. I think that Wallace Stevens was the
contemporary who most affected my writing then. But I got more
from Hopkins and the Metaphysical poets than I did from Stevens or
Hart Crane. I've always admired Herbert.

Interviewer: What do you like especially about Herbert?

Miss Bishop: To begin with, I like the absolute naturalness of tone.
Coleridge has some good remarks on this, you remember. And some
of Herbert's poems strike me as almost surrealistic, "Love Unknown" for instance. (I was much interested in surrealism in the
'30's.) I also like Donne, of course, the love poems particularly, and
Crashaw. But I find myself re-reading Herbert a great deal.

Interviewer: Do you owe any of your poems to Herbert?

Miss Bishop: Yes, I think so. "The Weed" is modelled somewhat
on "Love Unknown." There are probably others.

Interviewer: Do you have any comments on the religious poetry of
the '40's? I am referring especially to the long poems by Eliot and
Auden, also to such books as Tate's *The Winter Sea* and Lowell's
Lord Weary's Castle. In those days we seemed to be moving into
something rather unexpected, a brilliant period of Christian poetry.
But this has scarcely continued, has it?

Miss Bishop: As far as Eliot and Auden are concerned, I find Eliot
much easier to understand. He led up to the *Four Quartets* by a long
process. Eliot is not very dogmatic, not in his poetry (the prose is
another matter). Auden's later poetry is sometimes spoiled for me by
his didacticism. I don't like modern religiosity in general; it always
seems to lead to a tone of moral superiority. Of course I have the
greatest admiration for Auden as a poet. As for religious poetry and
this general subject, well, times have changed since Herbert's day.
I'm not religious, but I read Herbert and Hopkins with the greatest
pleasure.

Interviewer: Do you think it is necessary for a poet to have a "myth"—Christian or otherwise—to sustain his work?

Miss Bishop: It all depends—some poets do, some don't. You must have something to sustain you, but perhaps you needn't be conscious of it. Look at Robert Lowell: he's written just as good poetry since he left the Church. Look at Paul Klee: he had 16 paintings going at once; *he* didn't have a formulated myth to look to, apparently, and his accomplishment was very considerable. The question, I must admit, doesn't interest me a great deal. I'm not interested in big-scale work as such. Something needn't be large to be good.

Interviewer: But some poets and critics have been terribly concerned about this, haven't they?

Miss Bishop: Some people crave organization more than others—the desire to get everything in its place. Auden really thinks this way, I suppose. Marianne Moore, on the other hand, has no particular "myth," but a remarkable set of beliefs appears over and over again, a sort of backbone of faith.

Interviewer: I know you have a lively interest in the other arts—music and painting especially. Have your poems been much affected by these things?

Miss Bishop: I think I'm more visual than most poets. Many years ago, around 1942 or 1943, somebody mentioned to me something that Meyer Shapiro, the art critic, said about me: "She writes poems with a painter's eye." I was very flattered. All my life I've been interested in painting. Some of my relatives painted. As a child I was dragged round the Boston Museum of Fine Arts and Mrs. Gardner's museum and the Fogg. I'd love to be a painter.

Interviewer: What about "Songs for a Colored Singer"? You didn't compose those to tunes, as it were?

Miss Bishop: I was hoping somebody would compose the tunes for *them*. I think I had Billie Holiday in mind. I put in a couple of big words just because she sang big words well—"*conspiring* root" for instance. As for music in general: I'd love to be a composer! I studied counterpoint and the piano for years, and I suppose I'm still "musical." But I wanted to be a doctor, too, and I got myself enrolled at Cornell Medical School. I think Marianne Moore discouraged me from going on with that.

Interviewer: I wonder if you sometimes "feel" your way into a poem with a sense of its rhythms even before the subject has declared itself—you know, the way in which "Le cimetière marin" was composed?

Miss Bishop: Yes. A group of words, a phrase, may find its way into my head like something floating in the sea, and presently it attracts other things to it. I do tend to "feel" my way into a poem, as you suggest. One's mind works in unexpected ways. When I was writing "Roosters," I got hopelessly stuck; it just refused to get written. Then one day I was playing a record of Ralph Kirkpatrick performing Scarlatti: the rhythms of the sonata imposed themselves on me and I got the thing started again.

Interviewer: In composing a poem like this, do you start from a kind of pleasure in the stanzaic arrangement as such, or do you let the experience dictate the form?

Miss Bishop: In this case I couldn't say which came first. Sometimes the form, sometimes the subject, dominates the mind. All other poets I've ever talked to say pretty much the same thing. On this subject I rather like Housman's essay, *The Name and Nature of Poetry.* That's only one side of the question, but it's very well stated.

Interviewer: I wonder if you could reveal the *donnée* for your sestina called "A Miracle for Breakfast." It has an attractive surrealist quality about it, but I'm curious about the kind of experience which brought the poem into being.

Miss Bishop: Oh, that's my Depression poem. It was written shortly after the time of souplines and men selling apples, around 1936 or so. It was my "social conscious" poem, a poem about hunger.

Interviewer: That was the heyday of surrealism, too, wasn't it?

Miss Bishop: Yes, and I had just come back from my first year in France, where I had read a lot of surrealist poetry and prose.

Interviewer: When I read the poem here in Brazil, my students keep asking, "Was she waiting for the ferry?" You remember that early in the poem you have one crossing the river.

To move on to something else: "At the Fishhouses" is my favorite in your second book. This seems to me a kind of Wordsworthian poem, something like "Resolution and Independence." But your poem is mostly in the present tense and is more immediate and "existentialist." Wordsworth really seems to mean "emotion recollected in tranquillity'' and puts his poem mostly in the past tense. Do you have any comment on this comparison?

Miss Bishop: I think it's a question of how poetry is written. There has been a great change in the knowledge of, or at any rate the attitude towards, poetic psychology. One of the great innovators here is Hopkins. When I was in college I wrote a piece on him. While I was preparing it, I came across an essay on 17th Century baroque prose. The author—I've forgotten who—tried to show that baroque sermons (Donne's for instance) attempted to dramatize the mind in action rather than in repose. Applying this to Hopkins in the paper I was writing, I used a phrase which impressed me in "The Wreck of the Deutschland," where he says, "Fancy, come faster." He breaks off and addresses himself. It's a baroque poem. Browning does something like this, but not so strikingly. In other words, the use of the present tense helps to convey this sense of the mind in action. Cummings does this in some poems. Of course poets in other languages (French especially) use the "historical present" more than we do. But that isn't really the same device. But switching tenses always gives effects of depth, space, foreground, background, and so on.

Interviewer: Perhaps something like switching keys in music.

Miss Bishop: Yes, indeed, very much so.

Interviewer: What do you think about the dramatic monologue as a form—you know, when the poet assumes a rôle? This "poetry of experience" has been very attractive to a lot of poets. I believe you have done this two or three times—for instance in "Songs for a Colored Singer" and "Jerónimo's House."

Miss Bishop: I haven't given it much thought. Robert Lowell and others have done brilliant things in this form. I suppose it should act as a sort of release. You can say all kinds of things you couldn't in a lyric. If you have scenery and costumes, you can get away with a lot. I'm writing one right now.

Interviewer: I've just been reading a poem of yours called "A Summer's Dream." It's a wonderful miniature, an evocation of a dying seaside town. Every detail counts. Did you reduce this from something longer?

Miss Bishop: I went for the summer once to Cape Breton. This little village was very small indeed. I think in the poem I said the population contained a number of freaks. Actually there were a few more people. But some exceptional giants came from this region, and I think in the poem I conveyed some idea of what the people were like. No, I didn't compress the poem.

Interviewer: Do you find yourself revising a poem like this?

Miss Bishop: No. After a poem is published, I just change a word occasionally. Some poets like to rewrite, but I don't.

Interviewer: How did you happen to go to Key West, where you wrote some beautiful things? Did you find it a good place for writing?

Miss Bishop: In 1938, I believe, I was on the West Coast of Florida to fish. I went to Key West just for a couple of days to see what the fishing was like there. I liked the town and decided to go back there in 1939, after another eight months or so in Europe. Eventually I acquired a modest but beautiful old house. I can't say Key West offered any special advantages for a writer. But I liked living there. The light and blaze of colors made a good impression on me, and I loved the swimming. The town was absolutely broke then. Everybody lived on the W.P.A. I seemed to have a taste for impoverished places in those days. But my Key West period dwindled away. I went back for winters till 1949, but after the war it wasn't the same.

Interviewer: While I'm mentioning Key West, would you say something about John Dewey, whom you knew so well there? I think you'd agree that his prose style, even in his book on aesthetics, can be rather clumsy and does his reputation no good. But he was a very sensitive man, wasn't he?

Miss Bishop: Yes, very. I found him an adorable man. He could work under any conditions. Even at the age of eighty-five he missed no detail. He and Marianne Moore are the only people I have ever known who would talk to everyone, on all social levels, without the slightest change in their manner of speaking. I think this shows something important about Dewey and Marianne Moore—they have the kind of instinctive respect for other people which we all wish we could have but can only aspire to. No matter how foolish your question, he would always give you a complete and tactful answer. He loved little things, small plants and weeds and animals, and of course he was very generous in dealing with people. I remember when "Roosters" came out in *The New Republic;* he read it and said, "Well, Elizabeth, you've got these rhymes in threes very well. I wish I'd learned more about writing when *I* was young."

Interviewer: Some people might be surprised to know that Flannery O'Connor admired Dewey. The last time I saw her, in 1963, she was reading two of his books.

Miss Bishop: Well, I'm sure she knew more about his philosophy than I do!

Interviewer: You've been a literary associate of Robert Lowell's for quite a few years, haven't you?

Miss Bishop: I think, and I hope, we have been very good friends for twenty years. Both his life and his work have been of great importance to me. He is one of the few poets whose name in a table of contents or on the cover of a magazine gives me a sense of hopefulness and excitement even before I've read the poem.

Interviewer: What do you think of the turn his poetry has taken in the last few years—beginning with *Life Studies?*

Miss Bishop: One does miss the old trumpet blast of *Lord Weary's Castle,* but poets have to change, and possibly the more subdued magnificence of his later tone is more humane.

Interviewer: I think I have you about up to 1950 now. This would be the period when you had the appointment at the Library of Congress. You were there shortly after the Bollingen Prize fiasco, weren't you?

Miss Bishop: Léonie Adams was my predecessor, and she got the worst of that affair. MacLeish had a good idea about the job, and some of the poets fitted in rather well. I didn't really earn my keep—I didn't give lectures and readings, in fact never do. But for the only time in my life I saw bureaucracy functioning, and it certainly contributed to my education.

Interviewer: Like many literary people, you visited Pound during the '50's. Do you have any prose comment, as it were, to make about him? You've already put yourself on record in verse in "Visits to St. Elizabeth's."

Miss Bishop: I think I've said all I want to in that poem. I admired his courage enormously; he proved his devotion to literature during those thirteen years.

Interviewer: By the way, I'm rather interested in the formal scheme of that poem. How did you hit on it?

Miss Bishop: It's the old nursery rhyme, "This was the house that Jack built." I've always liked nursery rhymes, and this one seemed to work here.

Interviewer: Here in Brazil poets like Vinícius de Moraes have been

writing lyrics for *bossa nova*. Have you ever wanted to do something
like this in English?

Miss Bishop: I've always wanted to write popular songs, and I've
tried several times but never succeeded. I like some popular song
lyrics very much, "Mean to Me" for instance, and Ogden Nash's
"Speak Low."

Interviewer: I think quite a few people have already seen and
admired your new poem, the ballad called "The Burglar of Babylon."
It's a knockout. Did you have any trouble in finding a suitable medium
for this poem? It's really worked up from some journalistic material,
isn't it?

Miss Bishop: No, I sat down and wrote it almost straight off, with a
few additions and changes. Most of it was written in one day. It
naturally seemed to present itself as a ballad. It's a true story, taken
from the newspaper accounts; I made only two minor changes in
the facts.

Interviewer: Did you actually see Micuçu being hunted down on the
morro of Babylon in Rio?

Miss Bishop: No, but I saw the soldiers. We could watch them
through binoculars from the terrace of the apartment house.

Interviewer: With your new book of poems, *Questions of Travel,*
about to come out, what are your immediate literary plans?

Miss Bishop: Well, they are always the same, to write poems when
I can. I'm also planning a book of prose about Brazil. It is tentatively
called "Black Beans and Diamonds." It's to be a combination of a
travel book, a memoir, and a picture book. I am quite interested in
photography. I'd like to make Brazil seem less remote and less an
object of picturesque fancy. It's not really so far from New York. I
think that since the great naturalists (Darwin, Wallace, Bruce, and so
on) there hasn't been much close observation (at least by foreigners)
of Brazil. Except perhaps for Lévi-Strauss.

Interviewer: What do you think about the state of American poetry
right now?

Miss Bishop: Very good. We have lots of fine poets. Perhaps I'd
better not mention any names, but I really admire and read with
pleasure at least seven of my contemporaries. As far as poetry goes,
although I am afraid that is not very far, this is a period that I enjoy.

Poet Adds to List of Interesting Things

Dorothy Brant Brazier / 1966

From the *Seattle Times*, 25 February 1966, 21. Reprinted with permission of the *Seattle Times*.

Miss Elizabeth Bishop, who is teaching two of the late poet Theodore Roethke's courses at the University of Washington until June, is teaching for the first time in her life and is seeing the Western United States for the first time.

She has been busy doing other things, like writing three books of poetry and getting the 1956 Pulitzer Prize for one *(Poems: North & South—A Cold Spring),* covering the Amazon River by boat and buying and restoring an adobe house, circa 1720, in Ouro Prêto in the mining state of Minas Gerais, Brazil.

You can't do everything, so you choose the most interesting things to do. Miss Bishop now adds both teaching and seeing the West to her list.

Elizabeth Bishop, a name that is a household word with poets who have arrived and poets who are aspiring, was born in Massachusetts, lived in Nova Scotia as a small child and was educated at Walnut Hill School near Boston and at Vassar College.

Among her friends at Vassar was Mary McCarthy, the Seattle-born writer, who still has some family here.

In those days of the 1930's at Vassar, Miss Bishop briefly belonged to a mildly dissident gaggle of girl students who started an anonymous magazine in a Poughkeepsie speakeasy because they did not like the campus magazine. After three numbers of their magazine were published, they were asked to join the campus magazine staff—"it was a case of if you can't beat them, join them."

Miss Bishop has been writing since she was a little girl. During her last year of college she published poetry and a short story. The Pulitzer Prize was for her second book of poems. Her writings have been published in *Partisan Review, The Nation, The New Republic,*

The New Yorker, Encounter and *Poetry* Chicago. She has been consultant for poetry in the Library of Congress.

Since college, she has lived in New York, Washington and Paris,
and now we get to Brazil.

On a trip to Brazil in 1953, she suddenly became ill. After one bite
of the cashew fruit, she discovered she had a violent allergy to it and
for some time was near death.

You would think that would discourage further intimacy with the
country, but when Miss Bishop recovered, she discovered that Brazil
had a fascination for her as a place to live and work. Since then she
has made her home at Petrópolis, Brazil, in a modern house.

"It gets a little lively during the children's school vacation in
January, February and March," she said, "but it is a quiet place
despite the fact it is the seventh biggest city in Brazil. It's the place
where the court vacationed before the Republic and the summer
palace and the fantastic summer homes of the '70's and '80's are still
there and being used."

The ancient adobe house she bought recently in Ouro Preto is
"supposed to have a gold mine in the garden.

"It was owned by an old man who dug holes in every wall, looking
for treasure. There is a lot of land with a walled garden, a brook and
a waterfall, where they did gold-washing in the early days.

"There are 13 rooms of a primitive construction. The front walls
are a yard thick, like a fortress. The bamboo frames were tied together
with rawhide, which we discovered when we exposed a section, and I
am going to remove one wall to show this. There are a tile roof and
enormous beams. There are no cellars, of course, and you can walk
under the house. That's where they kept the donkeys.

"Great stones hold up the floors. I have discovered all kinds of
things—old branding irons, 30 old stirrups and the kind of candlehold-
ers they stuck in walls."

The house is being restored while she is here but she does not
expect the work to be finished before she gets home.

Miss Bishop hopes to spend two or three months a year in this
house. Her life in the old mining state will be as quiet as her life in
Petrópolis. She writes, does translating, reads and walks and feasts
her eyes on marvelous views. For a break, she goes to New York or,

in this case, to Seattle to get acquainted with today's college students. She likes them and they must like her. Some of them found her a place to live, moved her things and settled her—and you can't ask more than that of new-made friends in a strange town in the West.

Now Playing: A Touch of the Poetess

Tom Robbins / 1966

Reprinted from *Seattle Magazine* (April 1966), pp. 8–12.

There is no reason why poetry can't be as exciting as painting, music or films. There is, in fact, no reason why poetry can't be as exciting as football, drag-racing, armed robbery or statutory rape. There is no reason why it can't be, but it seldom is.

Perhaps the most exciting thing to happen in poetry in Seattle this year was the arrival here of a poet who is (incongruously) female, middle-aged, shy, soft-of-voice and pale as a winter moon. Her name is Elizabeth Bishop, and if her bearing seems more that of a librarian than a conjurer of exotic images, it should be noted that a young peyote-eating bohemian was encountered a few weeks ago on a University District corner avidly reading Miss Bishop's latest volume of verse and saying, "Man, there are some groovy trips in here."

Miss Bishop herself is a devotee of "trips," though not of the hallucinatory variety the hip young man had in mind. She has for more than 30 years roamed the far horizons of the earth, collecting colors and sounds and odors the way other travelers might acquire snapshots or souvenirs.

What with all her wandering and exploring, Miss Bishop's output of poetry has been modest—but notable. Her second collection of verse was published 12 years ago; called *Poems: North & South—A Cold Spring,* it contained just 48 works, but it won her a Pulitzer Prize. Her third volume was the recently published *Questions of Travel;* it has only 20 poems, but the book has attracted wide critical acclaim, including a nomination for this year's National Book Award.

When she came to Seattle in January to conduct a five-month poetry workshop at the U. of W., Miss Bishop left behind the kaleido-scopic charms of vast Brazil, where she has lived off and on since 1952. And she broke what, for a luminary in her profession, was an impressively long boycott of academia. "I'm the only American poet of my generation who has not earned his living as a teacher," Miss Bishop has said. "This is the first time that I have ever taught, and I hate, in a way, to have spoiled the record."

Because she has not lectured or instructed, because she has moved so infrequently in literary circles, Miss Bishop has naturally maintained a certain reticence about her craft. She has developed no theories about poetry; she has only written it. Perhaps, too, her absence from the campus, the clique and the cocktail circuit is partly responsible for the freshness and originality of her work.

"It never occurred to me to think what a poem might be," Miss Bishop remarks. "But now I've got to arrive at some definition, because any day one of my students might question me. Actually, theories about poetry are always made up after the fact. I don't think anyone ever sat down and wrote a poem according to a theory. If he did, it probably wasn't very good.

"One can't write poetry according to schedule. A good poem comes along seldom. Therefore, many poets develop theories in order to pass the time. W. H. Auden once said, 'Poets must have something to fill in the time. Otherwise, they fall so easily into dissipation.' " Miss Bishop was grinning, almost guiltily.

Her students at the U. of W. are amazingly bright, the new teacher has found, and many of them write good verse. Never having visited the Northwest before, she has been surprised by the almost exclusive concern of local poets, both students and professionals, with nature and the Orient. The nature poets Miss Bishop can accept as falling solidly in the English tradition of Wordsworth, but the Asian influences disturb her. She is a bit dismayed that so many of her students prefer to write *haiku,* the little 17-syllable Japanese vignettes.

"Maybe the *haiku* is not meant for our language," she muses. "We have a wealth of forms of our own that are suitable to our language. I mean English forms, not American. We're still more English than anything else, and this 'American language' which William Carlos Williams was always talking about is nonsense. We're writing better English poetry than the English are writing at present, so why not be proud of it? In English, *haiku* are quite unsatisfactory. They make me feel as if someone has pulled a chair out from under me. Give me the limerick any day."

The Beat poets of the fifties (Ginsberg, Ferlinghetti *et al*) had a profound influence on thousands of young people all over the world, but while Miss Bishop was generally in sympathy with the Beats' social revolution, she was less than enamored of their poetry. "Romantic and self-pitying," she calls it, and adds, "I hate self-pity poems." She is puzzled when one of her students submits a Ginsberg-like tirade. "Can you imagine these healthy milk-fed monsters commiserating with each other?" she asks. "The students here have it velvet. I'd recommend a trip to a really backward country for all American youth. When I think of the poor students I know in Brazil . . ."

(Miss Bishop realizes, of course, that affluence is not always a source of happiness. Quite the contrary. It can also create a spiritual poverty which is horrifying to behold—a greedy, smug indifference that forces many a sensitive poet to reach for his most poisonous adjectives. Still, when one considers the atrocious conditions in Brazil, where there is almost no middle class, just a handful of fabulously rich lording it over millions of desperately poor, one can appreciate Miss Bishop's lack of pity for America's physically comfortable young rebels.)

Brazil is the favorite topic of conversation with Miss Bishop, who was reared in New England and Nova Scotia, then educated at Vassar, where she, novelist Mary McCarthy and friends edited a renegade literary magazine from an "office" in a speakeasy. She has recently purchased a house in Ouro Prêto, a remote mountain town whose 18th-century Portuguese architecture has been perfectly preserved. In June, when her teaching assignment will have provided the extra funds needed to remodel the house, she will return to Ouro Prêto. But the poems she will leave here (*Questions of Travel* is enjoying a brisk sale in Seattle bookshops) will persist in evoking vivid visions of Brazil.

The 11 Brazilian poems which comprise the most interesting half of *Questions of Travel* may be compared to the paintings of Paul Gauguin. Like Gauguin, Miss Bishop has a keen, loving eye for the exotic: a born voyager's fondness for the unfamiliar detail which escapes the jaded notice of ordinary tourist and permanent resident alike.

Miss Bishop's imagery is extremely visual, and as a "colorist," she uses a palette that is both decorative and emotionally evocative. As unnaturalistic as Gauguin's, her hues are sharply defined and sumptuously rich. She writes of "red ground," "pink lightning," "blood-

black bromelias," a "milk-white sunrise" and moss that threatens
rocks "in lovely hell-green flames."

Her "surfaces" are smooth, flat and promiscuous of contour (also
like Gauguin), and whether she is writing in tight hot-panting rhyme
as in "The Burglar of Babylon," or in a free-flowing conversational
style, as in "The Riverman," her poems are filled with an atmosphere
of timeless calm and impregnated with a magical view of reality.

Consider the lines:

> The yellow sun was ugly
> Like a raw egg on a plate . . .

Or consider this passage from "The Riverman," a strange and mysterious account of an Amazonian villager who is learning to be a *sacaca,*
a witch doctor who specializes in water spirits:

> When the moon burns white
> and the river makes that sound
> like a primus pumped up high—
> that fast, high whispering
> like a hundred people at once—
> I'll be there below,
> as the turtle rattle hisses
> and the coral gives the sign . . .

Miss Bishop is a member of the poetry establishment, the polite
tradition; but her sense of wonder, her appetite for the magic and
marvelous in life, separates her from those others of the old guard
who, despite their Olympian reputations, are largely responsible for
the brown cloud of boredom which hangs heavily over American
verse.

Not long ago, David Wagoner, a U. of W. English professor and
himself a fine poet contributed to a Seattle newspaper an essay on the
subject, "Why People Hate Poetry." Children have a natural liking
for poems, Wagoner wrote, but, he contended, their enthusiasm is
swiftly turned to animosity by the dull, mechanical way in which
poetry is taught in most schools. Wagoner's theory is certainly valid,
but it is by no means the whole answer.

If poetry has a small audience, the fault is also that of the poets
themselves and, more specifically, of the journals which publish them.

More than any of the other arts, poetry has remained aloof from life.
It exists primarily in an academic atmosphere that is rarified, incestu-
ous and suffocating. The major poetry journals (usually affiliated with
universities) are strictly vegetarian—one can look through stacks of
them without finding a good raw piece of meat.

Poetry—our official poetry—has simply become too respectable.
And, in the arts, respectability is a form of paralysis, just as sentimen-
tality is a form of death. Poetry, as Baudelaire and Rimbaud and, yes,
Shakespeare, clearly demonstrated, is as much a part of the brothel
and the slaughterhouse as of the rose garden and the glade. If the
Beats did nothing else (among the other things they *did* do was to
spawn Gary Snyder, one of the most readable poets in the world
today), they took poetry out of the drawing room and shoved it back
in the streets where it belongs.

Although a poem should add up to something (that is, it should
begin at one point and move to another), intellectualized poetry, a
poetry of abstract ideas, cannot be expected to appeal to those
readers whose hearts and minds are open to life. The most successful
poem is one which is completely unexpected. If it does not provoke a
surprise or shock, and if it has not drawn more from imagination than
from technical skill, a poem cannot range much wider than the
dimensions of the page upon which it rests.

Elizabeth Bishop is not particularly interested in the public attitude
toward verse. "You can't teach anyone to write poetry," she has
said, "and you can't make people read it. If someone wants to read
poetry he'll find it, and if he wants to write it, you won't be able to
stop him. With all of the grants and paid readings, poets are better off
today than ever before—and perhaps that is what we should be
thankful for."

True, to some extent, but more often than not, grants, fellowships
and reading-tours are merely a means by which the academic establishment subsidizes mediocrity. What we should really be thankful for
is that there are a few poets with guts and fire and humor, and
imagination, a few poets who stand outside the pale, a few poets—and
Miss Bishop is one of these—who can still use the bright tools of
language to jimmy the lock on the door to paradise.

Elizabeth Bishop: Conversations and Class Notes

Wesley Wehr / 1966

The following comments by Elizabeth Bishop are from my conversations with her and from class notes taken during her 1966 poetry workshops at the University of Washington.

She had just arrived in Seattle from Brazil. The prospect of teaching a poetry class terrified her; she had never done such a thing before. But the University of Washington had made her a very good offer, and her house in Ouro Prêto needed a new roof.

It was January. It was pouring rain. Already she was desperately homesick. Every other day she was on the verge of cancelling the whole thing and going back to Brazil.

EB: I wish my students wouldn't spend so much time trying to "discover" themselves. They should let *other* people discover them. They keep telling me that they want to convey the "truth" in their poems. The fact is that we always tell the truth about ourselves despite ourselves. It's just that quite often we don't like how it comes out. If my students would concentrate more on all the difficulties of writing a good poem, all the complexities of language and form, I think that they would find that the truth will come through quite by itself.

There's another thing that bothers me very much: a tendency in my class for the students to write a kind of *mood* poem—about love, loss, dripping leaves, damp moonlight. Their poems are too vague. And if *anyone* in that class uses the word "communicate" *once* more, I'm going to *scream!* I *hate* that word! Those students are *not* there to "express" themselves; they're there to learn how to write a *good poem.*

I found out the other day, to my horror, that they don't even know the difference between a colon and a semicolon! Some of them speak so badly that I can't tell whether they're dumb or it's some kind of

local speech affectation or impediment. They keep saying things like,
"Oh, Miss Bishop, you *know* how it is." And I'll say, "No, I *don't*
know how it is. Why don't you tell me how it is? I'm not a mind
reader."

I asked them if any of them possibly knew what was wrong with
that *ghastly* slogan, *Winston Tastes Good Like a Cigarette Should?*
There was a complete silence in the classroom. I finally had to get out
my *Dictionary of English Usage* and slowly read to them the defini-
tions of *like* and *as*. When I got through, most of them were staring
blankly at me. I could have walked right out of the classroom at that
point. But I said, "If you students want so badly to *express* your-
selves, why don't you bother to learn even the simplest things about
your own language?" You studied with him—what did Theodore
Roethke do about this sort of thing? What was I brought here to
teach anyway?

EB: [to the class] Everyone in this class likes Shakespeare, and
after that, Dylan Thomas. But what about the seventeenth- and
eighteenth-century poets? And the nineteenth century? I was shocked
yesterday when you didn't spot those quotations from Keats, Tennyson, and Swinburne. We had a whole year of Wordsworth, Keats, and
Shelley when I was in high school. The romantics are still awfully
good poets. You *should* like Wordsworth. You're nature people here,
and I'd expect you to like him.

Have you read the Keats letters? I recommend them highly. I think
I enjoy them more than his poetry. He had a wonderful brain and a
very strong character. People wrote better letters in those days. Also,
you should read Hopkins's letters to Robert Bridges. They contain
some of the best statements I've ever read. His journals—for sheer
observations—are superb. He and Marianne Moore are the finest
observers I've ever read.

EB: You should use more *objects* in your poems—those things you
use every day . . . the things around you. Pop art has brought so
many things to our attention, whether we like them or not. One can
write very good poetry without vivid images, but I myself prefer
observation. I just don't find enough *things* in your poems. There are
so many things you students are not taking advantage of—alliteration,
for instance. My view from the fourteenth floor of the Meany Hotel

depressed me. I want you to write a poem, about thirty lines long, about Seattle. Here's a list of words to work in: viaduct, Space Needle, sea gull, "scenic drive" sign, cars. I'll give a special prize to whichever one of you manages to come up with the best rhyme for Seattle.

EB: [to the class, 5 January 1966, first day of class] I've gone through the poems which you handed in to me, and I've never seen so many *haikus* in my life. They're not very well written either. They're more like the sort of thing one might jot down when one is feeling vaguely "poetic."

Some of your rhymes are simply *awful!* And you seem to write a lot of free verse out here. I guess that's what you call it. I was rather appalled. I just couldn't scan your "free verse"—and one *can* scan Eliot. I think some of you are misled about free verse. It isn't that easy. Look at Eliot—you can scan his descriptive pieces about Cape Ann perfectly, and the same goes for *The Four Quartets* and *The Wasteland.* [She reads aloud a passage from *The Wasteland.*]

You see, you'd never take this for prose. It's *good* free verse. You can also look at E.E. Cummings and the rain poems of Apollinaire. But these poems of yours are spattered all over the page and I don't see any reason for it. I guess I'm rather old-fashioned.

I'm going to have to be very strict with you, I see. Let's do something like Housman for the first assignment. I just want something very *neat*—like a hymn. Some of you have good ears. I think it's a gift of God. But your sense of rhyme and form is atrocious. I'm going to be giving you some strict meter assignments, and later on we'll do something with iambic pentameter.

EB: You should have your head filled with poems all the time, until they almost get in your way.

A poet can't write poetry *all* the time. So when he isn't writing, there are various other things he can do: dissipation, or inventing theories about poetry, or writing his memoirs. It comes to about the same thing.

I would suggest you read one poet—*all* of his poems, his letters, his biographies, everything *but* the criticisms on him.

I believe in the fortunate accident, but you don't sit down and try

to have one. You have to be on the road before you can have
an accident.

When you imitate the old poets, you have a better chance of
sounding like yourself than when you're copying your contemporaries.

There's a Spanish proverb: a donkey who goes traveling comes
back still a donkey.

People seem to think that doing something like writing a poem
makes one happier in life. It doesn't solve anything. Perhaps it does
at least give one the satisfaction of having done a thing well or having
put in a good day's work.

EB: [to WW] All those students in my class—with their trusting
eyes and their clear complexions. Have you seen the expensive cars
that some of them drive? I don't know where they get all of their
money; perhaps their parents help them out. Most of them look quite
well fed and rather well off. And what do they write about in their
poems? *Suffering,* of all things! I don't think most of them know
anything about suffering, but their poems are just filled with it. I
finally told them that they should come to Brazil and see for themselves what *real* suffering is like. Then perhaps they wouldn't write
so "poetically" about it.

EB: I hardly know any of them, but I've already starting worrying
about some of my students. Going insane is very popular these days,
and it frightens me to see so many young people flirting with the idea
of it. They think that going crazy will turn them into better poets.
That's just not true *at all!* Insanity is a terrible thing . . . a *terrible*
thing! I've seen it first-hand in some of my friends, and it is not the
"poetic" sort of thing that these young people seem to think it is.
John Clare did *not* write glorious poetry while he was in the asylum,
I'm glad to say. I've known Marianne Moore extremely well over a
long time. Perhaps I'll tell my students about her some time—to show
them what can be drawn from such a relatively limited life as she has
had. I think it's important that my students start to know some of
these things. They have such narrow and sometimes destructive ideas
about what it is to be a poet. I've been thinking lately that I really
should say something to them about all of this. It's a very serious
matter.

EB: I've been fortunate from the start, winning prizes, having encouragement. Not that I've necessarily believed that I deserved it, but it's just happened that way. Sometimes I don't feel that I'm an especially good poet, but when I read some of the things that some of my contemporaries are writing, I guess I'm not so bad after all.

I've only had one rejection on a poem in my life. Somehow I always knew which poem to send to which magazine. But some of my students keep sending their poems to the most awful little poetry magazines. They seem to want so badly to be published that they just don't care where it is. I told them the other day that they shouldn't waste their time sending their poems to the bad little poetry journals. They should aim for the best ones. Some of these little magazines can be rather good at times, but so many of them will publish just about anything that's sent to them.

EB: I've never been one of those poets who will write a poem and then dash around showing it to everyone . . . pretending that they want criticism. Most of the times—in recent years anyway—I've usually known what was wrong with the poem. If I've shown my work to anyone for criticism, it's usually been to Cal Lowell or Miss Moore. Cal likes my new poem, the one I call *Poem*. He says it's very good. You can imagine how happy that made me.

EB: I *always* tell the truth in my poems. With *The Fish*, that's *exactly* how it happened. It was in Key West, and I *did* catch it just as the poem says. That was in 1938. Oh, but I did change *one* thing; the poem says he had five hooks hanging from his mouth, but actually he only had three. I think it improved the poem when I made that change. Sometimes a poem makes its own demands. But I always *try* to stick as much as possible to what *really* happened when I describe something in a poem.

WW: Elizabeth, do you ever lose your motivation?

EB: Lose my motivation? You ask me the oddest questions. Let me put it this way. I would say that sometimes my "motivations" will come *back* for a day, maybe even for *two* days. And then I really have to get down to work! That happened to me a few weeks ago. I suddenly felt very "motivated," as you call it. I cleaned the kitchen oven and finally answered some letters. Is that what you mean about being motivated? Or did you mean do I have sudden fits of inspiration to write poems? Oh, I *hope* you didn't mean something like *that!* I haven't been able to write a single good line in Seattle. Once or twice most of a poem has come to me all at once, but usually I write very, very slowly.

EB: Because I write the kind of poetry that I do, people seem to assume that I'm a *calm* person. Sometimes they even tell me how *sane* I am. But I'm not a calm person at all. I can understand how they might think that I am, but if they really knew me at all, they'd see that there are times when I can be as confused and indecisive as anyone. There are times when I really start to wonder what holds me together—awful times. But I feel a responsibility, while I'm here at least, to *appear* calm and collected . . . so these young people won't think that *all* poets are erratic.

EB: Did you read what that interviewer wrote about me? What was his name? . . . oh, yes . . . Tom Robbins. He described me as looking and acting like some schoolmarm. That really hurt my feelings a bit. I used to be quite a tomboy. I was *very* good at climbing trees, and did all sorts of wild things. And then they wanted a photograph of me to accompany the magazine interview. I *hate* being photographed. The only photograph that's ever been taken of me which I rather like is one where I'm on a bear rug going "Goo, goo!" at the camera. That one I don't mind at all. I'm just not photogenic, and never have been.

EB: Some of our critics can find something in common between just about anything. Comparing me with Wittgenstein! I've never even read him. I don't know *anything* about his philosophy. Have you read Gombrich's *Art and Illusion?* He says all art comes from art. My own favorite reading is Darwin.

EB: I'm just back from giving a poetry reading in the Southwest. I didn't want to do it at all, but they *do* pay rather well down there. When I finished reading the first poem, the audience clapped so enthusiastically. I read another poem, and they clapped even louder. I began to feel like some singer . . . like Judy Garland. All that applause! They really seemed to be enjoying it, and, to my dismay, I started to enjoy it myself. I'm afraid I may have a bit of the ham in me—more than I realized. Oh, I hope this isn't a bad sign.

EB: I had some psychiatry once—when it was fashionable to do that sort of thing, and some friends of mine had told me to try it. It didn't help me especially to understand myself any better, but it certainly helped me to understand some of my friends.

WW: Do I have too many defenses?
EB: Too *many?* Can one ever have *enough* defenses?

EB: One evening I was walking down Lexington Avenue, feeling bored and perhaps even a bit sorry for myself. I hadn't seen anyone for several days, and no one had telephoned me. The only mail I'd received had been a few bills and circulars. I'd just had to get out of my apartment for a while. Then, of all things, I ran into Virgil Thomson. *He* was out for a walk—looking every bit as bored and down in the dumps as I was. Somehow that snapped me right out of it. The very thought that someone as brilliant and famous as Virgil Thomson could look so bored and at loose ends too quite cheered me up.

WW: Elizabeth, I need to ask you for some advice about love [she came to the kitchen doorway and stared incredulously at me].
EB: You want to ask me a question about W-h-a-t? Did you say it was about *love?* What would *ever possibly* give you the idea that *I* of *all* people would know *anything* about a thing like *that?* If you ever were to know much about my personal life, you certainly wouldn't come to *me* for any sagely advice about a thing like love. I've usually been as confused about it as just about anyone else I've known. If you really are concerned about that subject, I'd suggest that you go and read Auden. If *he* doesn't know something about love, I just don't know who else does. . . .
[Later that afternoon, after we had finished some shopping and were walking down University Way, she stopped and turned to me.] Wes, I'm awfully sorry that I dodged your question the way I did. It took me by surprise, and I just didn't know how I should answer it. But I've been thinking about it, since you did ask me. And I will say *this* much: if any happiness ever comes your way, GRAB IT!

EB: Léonie Adams is very serious. I think she may feel that I'm rather frivolous. Do go to her class. She'll have good things to say.
Have you heard from Léonie lately—or had any news of her? She's

very intelligent and someone you would do well to listen to. She knows what she's talking about.

WW: I've been trying to read some of the "confessional" poets lately.

EB: Don't you have anything better to read than that? I'm really quite surprised at you. I *hate* confessional poetry, and so many people are writing it these days. Besides, they seldom have anything interesting to "confess" anyway. Mostly they write about a lot of things which I should think were best left unsaid. Dear, now you've got me a bit worried about your tastes in reading matter. Maybe I'd better send you some old copies of the *National Geographic*.

WW: I need to ask you about what I eventually should do with the letters you've sent to me . . . would it be all right for me to donate them to some library or archive? They could be restricted, of course.

EB: Don't *give* them to any library—that would be sentimental. You should sell them instead—and ask a good price for them, if you can get it. You may need the money some day, and then you'd regret having given them away.

That reminds me: a while ago I was in a little bookshop in Greenwich Village. There was a book I wanted to buy, but I didn't have enough money on me. So I asked the proprietor if I could make out a check. When he looked at the check, he asked me if I were Elizabeth Bishop the *poet*. I said yes. He said, "Miss Bishop, I've been making some money off of you lately. I've just sold one of your letters for $100. It was a short one . . . typed and with a handwritten postscript. And I sold another letter of yours for $125 not long ago." I had been writing and mailing letters most of that morning, and I had no idea they were so valuable. But I don't understand why you think that they should be restricted. I can pretty well remember what I've written to you, and I don't recall anything that should be restricted.

WW: Well, for instance, in one of them you write something like, "Another book by R.—the thought of it makes me shudder!"

EB: I certainly would stand by that remark. You don't have to be so protective of me. Was there anything else I wrote that concerns you?

WW: You called Sam F. an idiot.

EB: But he *is* an idiot!

Post Script

[Several weeks before she died I phoned Elizabeth in Boston.
During the conversation, I mentioned that I had taken notes on some
of the things that she had said to me and in class, and I read her a few
of them.]

EB: They sound like things I might have said, but I don't remember
having said some of them. I'm glad you wrote them down. Some of
those remarks are actually rather good. Would you mind sending me
a copy of them? If some day I run out of things to say, I just may start
quoting myself.

Ouro Prêto: Springtime at the Winter Festival

Visão / 1969

Excerpted from *Visão* (São Paulo) (Aug. 1, 1969), pp. 50–51.

In July, Ouro Prêto awakens as if from a long sleep. The ancient stones, quiet and heavy with memory, flourish once again, unexpectedly, in the light of a thousand colored costumes, and the saints in their gilded cupolas smile at the sound of new voices, fresh voices. It is springtime because there is youth. En mass, in rushes, down the hillsides, sitting on the sidewalks, in the plazas, in the churches. Laughing, singing, painting, living and learning, avid students pour in from all the Brazilian states, from Uruguay, Argentina, and even the U.S.A. And after them, come tourists, by the hundreds.

The only ones who do not attend the Ouro Prêto Festival are those who do not want to come or do not know about it. Sponsored by the Federal University of Minas Gerais, the State Government, and the Mayor's office of Ouro Prêto, this year's festival will cost around 200 thousand "cruzeiros novos," but it will cost the tourist nothing. Concerts, theater, exhibitions—are free, informal, and open to all. The students enrolled in courses pay a mere 200 "cruzeiros novos" to cover housing and meals. In 1967 the students numbered 269, in 1968, 308, and this year, close to four hundred. There is housing to suit every pocketbook—from a hotel like the Pouso do Chico Rei (with its refined good taste and comfort, thanks to the magic of Lili Corrêa de Araújo, that Danish darling and artist of Ouro Prêto) where a luxurious room, including breakfast, costs 40 "cruzeiros novos" a day, down to "student houses," where meals and a room run from 8 to 10 "cruzeiros novos" a day.

Attending the Festival was this reporter for *Visão.* He took in ballets, heard the bands, and watched the "capoeiras." He was much moved by what he saw at the Municipal Theater, in the churches and sacristies. He talked with young people, asked the old ones questions, ate in the sparkling clean "bandejão" of the Academic Center of the

47

School of Minas, where a wholesome, plentiful meal costs 3 "cruzeiros novos." And he patronized the bars, particularly Chicão's "XPTO," that institution where the whole city meets after the theaters let out.

Elizabeth Bishop is an old friend of Brazil and things Brazilian. Considered to be one of the greatest of American poets of the day, she won the Pulitzer Prize for poetry in 1959, after having lived here for some time.

"I made my first trip to Ouro Prêto in 1952, before they had built the new highway. It used to take three days to get here. Later I began to come here regularly, some seven or eight times. Some four years ago I bought a house in which I intend to live three or four months a year with the rest of the time in the U.S.A."

P: "What does Ouro Prêto mean to you?"

B: "I do not know. I simply like it. It is small, but it is a city of truth, vitality. I like its architecture very much, I like its churches. There is something in this city's character that agrees with me."

P: "Is the past's presence felt in Ouro Prêto?"

B: "No, I don't think so. Only a very few of the more educated people sense that. It's a shame. Many complain of the Historical Heritage people and say that if it were not for their meddling Ouro Prêto would today be a city . . . 'a city as good as Belo Horizonte!' I fear that its inhabitants, at least some of them, do not sufficiently appreciate their city."

P: "Artists continue to stream in. Is there a literary ambience, an artistic movement in Ouro Prêto?"

B: "It is difficult to say. An amusing case. Two years ago I was staying at the Pouso do Chico Rei. So was Vinícius de Moraes. It was summertime, but cold and rainy, and Vinícius, Lili and I were sitting in the pantry. We took to reading detective stories, the entire afternoon. We didn't exchange a single word. Thereupon *O Globo* from Rio published an article headed: 'An Intellectual Movement in Ouro Prêto,'" along with a picture of the back part of my house, which seemed to be falling to pieces."

P: "Elizabeth, if you had a lot of money or running the government" [she interrupts, laughingly: "What government?"], "what would you like to do for Ouro Prêto?"

B: "If I were Rockefeller, for example? I would reconstruct everything correctly and I would also knock down many of the ugly things, the bad modern construction that was thrown up. I would improve the hospitals and the clinics, I would provide the poor with more medicine free of charge. My house is the only house in Ouro Prêto that has a septic system; I would build a sewage system. I would also plant trees throughout the city and I would try to create a green belt around the city."

P: "Many say that they would like to construct a satellite city for the people and turn Ouro Prêto over to the artists. What do you think of the idea?"

B: "I think it is nonsense. In the first place, there aren't many artists. It would become a ghost city. One of the things I like about it is that it is still a city, not a dead place. It is one of those cities, rare in the world, in which the "crazies" can still live free and even earn a living. Besides, I would hate living in a city inhabited solely by artists. I would leave it in a rush. One artist to a block is more than enough. Artists shouldn't get too close to one another or heap up excessively. One thing I am sorry about. There was a café in the city, across from the movie-house, but it is no longer there. It does people good just to sit and rest, to look around at other people, before going home.

"This is the first of these festivals that I have attended and I haven't seen much of it. Some old films. I was somewhat disappointed in some of them. I know it must all be very difficult to do—movie-house, technical details, etc. But, bit by bit, it will improve. The city becomes noisier, but that doesn't bother me, for good things do happen. Yesterday I heard the band. I like bands very much and I find that the Ouro Prêto band is as good as any of the other bands. As a matter of fact, we have three very good bands. It is nice to hear the band on Sundays, with the fireworks and all.

"The festival that is going on is principally a festival of music and the plastic arts. It would have been interesting had Carlos Drummond de Andrade been present. After all, he is the poet of Minas."[1]

---

1. Quotes the first twelve lines from Bishop's poem "Under the Window: Ouro Preto."

Poetry as a Way of Life

Regina Colônia / 1970

Reprinted from *Jornal do Brasil* (Rio de Janeiro) (June 6, 1970), p. 8.

The enormous house was built at the end of the eighteenth century. In the kitchen a small woman is busily baking a torte for dinner. She has rolled up her sleeves to her elbows, and her hands are white with wheat flour. She kneads her dough with determination. Behind her, windows open out to the valley, to the churches and houses of Ouro Prêto.

"The only problem in my being basically a North-American poet and, at the same time, living in Brazil," she says, "is that the mails are not very good."

But Elizabeth Bishop is more than merely a North-American poet. She is, according to the critics, one of the greatest poets of contemporary literature. Among her many prizes there is a Pulitzer, and this year, the National Book Award.

The West Indies, Newfoundland, and Mexico are among the places in which Elizabeth Bishop—born in New England in 1911—lived before coming to Brazil.

"Of Ouro Prêto I love above all the things that are made here. The furniture, the implements of the eighteenth century are solid. The classical does not appeal to me. What matters is durability—here things last."

I write, seated at the kitchen table. Beside me, from the tiled wall, hangs a bunch of garlic. *Here things last*. "Solidity" and "survival" are constants in whatever Elizabeth says, the result of a process in which, to safeguard the essential, many other things become secondary.

"In poetry words are the most important thing," she says. "All ideas are concentrated in them. What lasts is the poem and not what has motivated it. A woman should never permit herself to wax emotional over a poem written for her; a poet's thought is always much more concerned with the manner in which he composes a poem than with the woman (as a person) who inspired it."

In the living room, there is next to the fireplace an excellent
example of those gargoyles used by the boatmen on the Rio São
Francisco. Elizabeth traveled in Amazonas, by way of the São Francisco, stopping in Salvador, Diamantina, Cabo Frio, and Parati.
  "When I travel my principal interest is not people. What really
appeals to me is scenery and architecture."
  Robert Lowell, the great North American poet and her friend for
more than 25 years, once wrote: "She is too powerful for mismanaged
fire and too civilized for idiosyncratic incoherence. When we read
Elizabeth Bishop, we enter the classical serenity of a new country."
  Elizabeth has published *North & South—A Cold Spring* (which
earned her a Pulitzer in 1955), *Questions of Travel,* and *The Complete
Poems*—for which she received, in 1970, a National Book Award.
  "Writing poetry is a *way of life,* not a matter of testifying but of
experiencing. It is not the way in which one goes about interpreting
the world, but the very process of sensing it. When one is 'on the
move,' one obviously *discovers* things, but that is merely part of the
process. That's why poetry can eventually transmit some sort of
experience to the reader, but that is far from being its purpose. That's
also why poetry cannot influence the destiny of a people. Despite the
fact that good poetry always reflects a certain attitude toward contemporary history, there are things missing in it that keep it from
functioning as *propaganda.*"
  Elizabeth wears a pink shirt and "American" slacks. Her hair is
white but her gray eyes are extremely bright.
  "The age we live in, with its terrible *boom* in mass communications,
has things about it that endanger poetry as we know it. Nevertheless,
I believe that there are well-founded hopes that poetry will not suffer
the horrors that have already been visited on music and painting, for
example—music by means of radio and tape-player and painting
through an advanced technology of multiplication that permits anyone
to have at home a Van Gogh or a Picasso. And therein lies the great
danger—the means of communication have to such an extent facilitated the diffusion of the messages, be they art or not, that nowadays
people no longer know how to see or listen.
  "Down through the ages, poetry has been expressly spared for two
good reasons. First, writing poetry does not pay, or when it does pay,
it pays little. (The result is that only those who want to write poetry

for its own sake continue with the genre.) Secondly, very few people read poetry, something which has enabled it to escape popularity and vulgarization. Thus poetry has evaded the distortions that it might have undergone.

"And even in the event that the modes of mass communication were to spread poetry as widely as they have popular music, there would emerge in all probability an underground—as in the seventeenth century—in which poems would once again be written on single sheets of paper to be distributed to a limited number of readers.

"Today the best market for poetry is really North America," says Elizabeth. "There is great enthusiasm for it in the universities, one senses. I myself have taught 'Verse Writing' and 'Contemporary Poetry' at the University of Washington, in Seattle. And there is a great flowering in contemporary poetry. Of the older generation, Robert Lowell and Marianne Moore stand out—the latter, in fact, I consider to have made the greatest and most original contributions to twentieth-century poetry. In the younger generation, there are James Merrill and John Berryman—both being more overtly political.

"As for concrete poetry, I like only Cummings—a brilliant and good humored poet, one who really had something to say. Concrete poetry that other poets make, I find uninteresting. It has only an initial impact—a word game, at times amusing and witty, but useless and impossible to remember.

"In France I like the poets Char and Michaux. In Brazil, João Cabral and Drummond—I do not believe that there is any exceptional quality in the younger ones. The best poets of today seem to me to be the North Americans. As to the greatest North American poet—I am reminded that once when Gide was asked who in his opinion was the greatest poet in the French language, he responded: 'Victor Hugo, alas!' I would say that, in my opinion, the greatest North American poet is Whitman, alas!"

A violent allergic reaction to the cashew forced Elizabeth Bishop to stay in Brazil. In 1952, she was visiting Brazilian friends she had met in Chicago during the war. Her intention was to go on to Argentina. But her illness caused her to change her plans: she stayed for eighteen months. Since then she has lived mostly in Brazil—first in Petrópolis, then Rio, and since last year, Ouro Prêto.

Currently Elizabeth is preparing a book that collects her prose texts

on Brazil and an anthology of Brazilian poetry to be published in two
volumes in the United States. In her *Complete Poems* she includes
her translations of poems by Drummond and João Cabral. Her *Diary
of Helena Morley* is a translation of *Minha Vida de Menina*. She has
also translated stories by Clarice Lispector, published articles about
Brazil in the *New York Times,* and prepared a book on Brazil for *Life*
magazine's "Foreign Lands" series.

"In the United States a system of cash grants to writers helps a
good deal," she says, "saving them time that otherwise would be
spent in teaching or doing some other kind of work to support
themselves. You earn to write and you choose your publisher. For
example, the Rockefeller Foundation grant that I received for 1966–67
amounted to 6000 U.S. dollars a year (twenty-seven thousand 'cruzeiros novos').

"There are critics who rank me as *the greatest feminine poet of the
decade.* That's simply ridiculous! What does what I do have to do
with the term *feminine?* Men and women do not write differently. In
the United States, for example, the best of contemporary prose-
writers is a woman—Flannery O'Connor—recently deceased.

"But, evidently, there are those still who judge us prejudicially
along those romantic lines. Yet one must take those persons with a
touch of humor because, if not, one will embitter life itself. In any
case, things are changing very rapidly. In the United States the
younger generation has already achieved equality between the sexes.
My students, for example, were tremendous. And all over the whole
world, generally speaking, there is the tendency to transcend such
prejudice. In Latin America it may still take a while, but things
will change."

This affirmation brings to mind the words of a North American
critic, Philip Booth, on the subject of Elizabeth's poetry. "Miss
Bishop looks at the world with an eye so individual that to share her
vision is—gratefully—to revise one's own. She is one of the few true
poets of this, or any other, hemisphere."

Pulitzer Prize-winning Poet Visits UW

Eileen Farley / 1974

Reprinted from the *University of Washington Daily*, 28 May 1974.

Being a woman is no handicap to gaining recognition as a poet, according to Pulitzer Prize winner Elizabeth Bishop. "But it sometimes makes one dubious of the recognition one does get," she explained.

"It's not a question of recognition, it's a question of criticism given. Criticism of women poets is often very unfair," the 63-year-old poet said.

"You read a very favorable review of a writer, saying she is very clever and talented and you think this writer must be wonderful. Then, at the end, it says 'Best book written by a woman,' and all that has gone before loses its value."

Besides the Pulitzer Prize, Bishop has received a Guggenheim fellowship, the Shelley Memorial Award and a $5,000 grant from the American Academy of Poets Award.

She taught here in 1966 and 1973 as the visiting poet and was on campus last week to give the eighth annual Roethke Memorial Reading. She is the first woman to read for the memorial series.

"I'm not a flaming militant," Bishop said concerning feminism. When she first began being published in the thirties, however, she refused to be in women's anthologies. "I always refused as my own form of protest then."

Bishop still refuses to be published in women's anthologies.

"Now people think I'm being an elitist. But I like my anthologies, all the arts, mixed: sexes, colors and races. Art is art and should have nothing to do with gender."

The annual Roethke Memorial reading is given in honor of Theodore Roethke, who taught here from 1947 until his death in 1963. Like Bishop, Roethke received a Pulitzer. He also received two Guggenheim fellowships.

54

At the Memorial Reading, besides reading her own poems, Bishop read three of Roethke's, commenting on some of the philosophy behind his work. She also spoke about her personal acquaintanceship with Roethke.

"On a few occasions Roethke would come into town (New York) and we drank champagne together," she said. "After one of these champagne parties he called me the next day. He said he had to catch some special train to Seattle and 'would I help him pack?' He said he'd never make it to the station otherwise. I went up to his hotel room and there were dozens of shirts and pajamas scattered about and one of the biggest suitcases I've ever seen . . .

"I worked on that while he collected his papers. We got to Grand Central just as his train was being called. He kissed me goodbye and said 'You're a quick kid in a caper.' "

While re-reading his poems and notebooks and preparing last week's reading, Bishop said she noticed three things about Roethke. She said he was musical, metrical and rhythmical, even in free verse; that he believed in forms as useful practice in writing and that he was "pro-poetry."

Bishop said that much of the poetry by young writers today is either cynical or ironic. "Somebody has labelled it anti-poetry," she said.

"Of course, it is nothing new," Bishop said. She cited e. e. cummings' poem about the Roman forum ("Consider, darling, yon busted statue") as "very different from Lord Byron's 'Roman Forum.' "

"I'm not against it (irony). One is often compelled to use it. But you get freshmen and sophomores writing bitter, wry comments . . .

"Anti-poetry can become just as tiresome as Wordsworth and the beauties of Nature."

"Unlike most contemporaries, Roethke wrote 'straight' poetry. I think he was really 'pro-poetry.' He's unashamedly poetic—beautiful and musical."

Bishop said she thought Roethke considered teaching as important as writing. But she said, "I don't enjoy teaching as much as writing. I teach to earn a living. I probably shouldn't say that. I like the students very much, but if someone gave me a million dollars, I wouldn't teach."

Bishop's first teaching position was the one she held here in 1966.

"I came to this hotel (University Tower—then Meany Hotel)," she said. "The rain never stopped and I didn't know a soul. That first morning, before the first class of my life, was the worst. But the students were very nice and very friendly."

Bishop said she doesn't think about whom she is trying to communicate with when she writes a poem. "You're just thinking about the poem (or should be)," she said. "Your thoughts and feelings are on the tip of the pen. I suppose propaganda poets are thinking of their propaganda, but they rarely seem to write good poetry that way."

"The mysterious thing about any art is that other people do understand (what you're trying to say)."

Bishop said she's never completely satisfied with a poem. "But I try something else. They never really come up to the poem you had in mind."

Bishop has received a great many awards: Consultant in Poetry at the Library of Congress 1949–50, the Houghton Mifflin poetry fellowship award, a Guggenheim Fellowship, the Shelley Memorial Award, the Pulitzer, an Amy Lowell Fellowship, an award of $5,000 from the Academy of American Poets and the Order of Rio Branco from the Brazilian government.

She said it was especially nice to receive the Pulitzer and the National Book Award while in Brazil. She felt perhaps it had kept people from thinking she lived in Brazil because she couldn't make it in her own country.

Her attitude toward receiving these literary honors might be summed up in the story she tells about one reaction she got after receiving the Pulitzer. "When I got the Pulitzer (in 1956 while living in Brazil) there was a lot of fuss. My picture in the papers, and so on."

She said that when a friend went to the market to buy vegetables the vendor mentioned seeing the picture and sent his congratulations. Then, according to her friend, he boasted, "All my customers are so lucky. The other day Senhora So-and-so up the street bought a ticket in the lottery and she won a bicycle."

Bishop, who lived in Brazil for over 15 years, does not plan on returning there to live. "I get homesick (for Brazil) but now I have come back to live in my own country."

Book and Author: Elizabeth Bishop

Anna Quindlen / 1976

From the *New York Post*, 3 April 1976, 33. Copyright © *New York Post*. Reprinted with permission from the *New York Post*.

Elizabeth Bishop didn't have much. Her father died when she was an infant, her mother went mad a few years later. There were the two sets of grandparents, one pair in Massachusetts, the other in Nova Scotia, with whom she spent her holidays. There was boarding school, and Vassar. Always there was the poetry; finally there was Marianne Moore.

"I wanted to study medicine," she recalled, this woman poet with the leonine head of a prime minister on small shoulders. "But when I'd gotten out of college I'd already published several things and—and I think Miss Moore discouraged me [from taking up medicine].

"The college librarian arranged for us to meet. I came to New York and met her on the left-hand bench in the Reading Room of the Public Library. I was scared out of my wits, but it went very well. We became very good friends for more than 30 years. Thirty years? Yes, she died three, no, four years ago."

So Elizabeth Bishop, now 65, practiced poetry instead of medicine, and practiced it very well. She won many of the awards her friend Miss Moore did, including the Pulitzer Prize. Now she has added another to her list: the fourth $10,000 Neustadt prize for literature, which is being awarded for the first time to a woman and an American.

"About every nine or ten years I seem to produce a book," said Miss Bishop, sitting in the corner of a patterned sofa at the Cosmopolitan Club—"very genteel," she whispers in the lounge—and tapping the carpet impatiently with a cane forced upon her by a pulled ligament.

"I never dreamed I'd receive this, but apparently they're going to make me earn it. I have to read—twice, I think—and I'm supposed to make a speech. I've never made a speech in my life and I don't think

I can. Then I get a silver eagle's feather.'' She laughed. "It's supposed
to stand for manliness. 'But in your case it will be womanliness,' they
told me.''

The prize seems fitting. Miss Bishop's poetry tends toward vivid,
imaginative descriptions of nature, often carefully rhymed and me-
tered, with the lessons implicit in the verse. "I think geography comes
first in my work,'' she said, "and then animals. But I like people, too;
I've written a few poems about people.''

Two of them were written for fellow poets. "I'd been asked to write
a piece of prose about Ezra Pound and I'd tried and tried and I
couldn't.'' Instead she produced "Visit to St. Elizabeth's,'' a poem
with the cadence of the children's verse about the house that Jack
built. In the same way she wrote "Invitation to Miss Marianne
Moore,'' as much a paean to New York as to the woman "for whom
the agreeable lions lie in wait on the steps of the public library.''

Others of her poems are about Brazil, where Miss Bishop lived
from 1951 until 1967. Now she lives on the water in Boston and
teaches at Harvard, "I was very proud—for a long time I was the only
American poet who didn't teach. But it was a question of money.''

Her students sometimes delight, sometimes disappoint her. "It's a
truism, it's in all the Sunday supplements, but I'm shocked at how
little my students have read. My contemporaries, those that are still
alive, are extremely well read. The really youngest generation now
tends to write in free verse, but it seems to me that the best poets set
themselves some strict limitations. Wallace Stevens almost never got
away from iambic pentameter.

"And Robert Lowell said in the last letter I had from him that he's
going back to form, that he was tired of the loose free verse he
was writing.''

Her influences? "The English metaphysical poets, mainly George
Herbert, he's my favorite. And then in college Wallace Stevens. And
then, of course, Marianne Moore.''

Reading Scares Poet Bishop

Jim Bross / 1976

Reprinted from the *Norman Transcript*, 11 April 1976, 1.

Elizabeth Bishop, just a few hours before receiving the 1976 Books Abroad-Neustadt International Prize for Literature in ceremonies at the University of Oklahoma Friday evening, confessed to fright.

"I'm going to read my poetry there tonight," she confirmed with an abbreviated shudder and only a trace of humor. "I don't do that very often. It, uh, scares me."

The 65-year-old poet is improving. Seven or eight years ago she'd have been "scared to death." For many, many years Bishop was one of the few, perhaps the single, noted American poet who refused to travel about the country lecturing.

She won the Pulitzer Prize for her poems in *A Cold Spring*. She picked up a National Book Award for *Complete Poems*.

The demands, the pressures for personal appearances and readings mounted. Bishop, ever polite, refused.

Then, in 1969, she did a little turnabout and scheduled some of her first lectures in 23 years. "It was the money," she admits.

Bishop scheduled a few more appearances in following years. She came to OU in 1973 as a visiting artist in the Contemporary Authors Series. She insists she had a "good time with a good audience."

The audience must have been at least as receptive here Friday evening, when she received her $10,000 prize. For the first time those familiar with Bishop around here can remember, she allowed herself to be photographed. And, if Bishop experienced any fear during her reading, it was a private one.

"I'm getting use to it—the readings," she allowed earlier Friday. The photographs are something else. They were allowed only during the presentation ceremonies.

It's not an offensive modesty that leads Bishop to turn down photographs and limit appearances. Encounters with her are pleasant, conversational affairs. She speaks enthusiastically about her travels, a passion that has taken her to most of the world's ports and feeds her writing. Other writers or mutual acquaintances spark animated discourse with Bishop.

It surprises them, that "reticient" is the word most often tossed about in describing the poet. "It surprises me, too," she says.

"I don't know. Maybe it's because I don't write any confessional poetry."

Bishop doesn't write about Bishop, although her poetry and short stories often are referred to as "unusually personal and honest in wit, perception and sensitivity." The writing focuses upon those "special sights and events . . . ," as John Ashbery, the American poet who co-nominated her for this prize, notes.

Bishop is on the move almost every year, collecting those creative forces. The title of her most recent book of poetry, *Geography III,* accurately reflects her artistic fascination. "Actually, I feel rather countryless," she says with no hint of regret.

Bishop says she'd "go just about anywhere if anybody would give me a ticket." About the only places she hasn't been are the Arctic and Antarctic. But, she's "dying" to get there.

Bishop was born in New England, but moved to Nova Scotia to live with an aunt after being orphaned at 5. Nova Scotia, she recalls with characteristic regional sensitivity, "is smaller than New England and much more understandable to a child's mind."

She presently makes her home near the harbor in Boston—the city in which she published her first poems while editing a boarding school magazine.

Bishop published her first poems professionally, that is for pay, while in college at Vassar. There, she, novelist Mary McCarthy and other classmates established a literary magazine.

That first professional effort earned $35, "or something like that," Bishop remembers.

"In general," she says, "I don't know any poet who could live on what they earn. Not at first, anyway. I suppose that's good. No one is going into poetry to make money.

"I've been lucky that way. After I published my first book of poetry (*North & South,* winner of the Houghton Mifflin Co. Poetry Award), fellowships and other types of support seemed to come in at the proper times.

"It's kept me off the lecture circuit. Some of my friends have wound up in the hospital doing those lectures. It's killing.

"After tonight (Friday), it's home to Boston for me. Then, maybe soon, another trip somewhere."

A Conversation with
Elizabeth Bishop
J. Bernlef / 1976

Reprinted from *Het ontplofte gedicht: Overpoëzie [The Ex-
ploded Poem: About Poetry]* (Amsterdam: Em. Querido's Uit-
geverrij B.V., 1978), pp. 84–92.

Seeing someone you admire for the first time always brings with it a
curious confusion. On Wednesday the 16th of June, in Rotterdam, at
half past two p.m., I entered the hotel where the poets that partici-
pated in the annual Poetry International were staying and saw her
sitting in the lobby: Elizabeth Bishop, an American poetess I had
wanted to interview in 1971. At that time she didn't come because she
was ill with dysentery in Brazil. Feeling that "one never knows,"
however, I had carefully kept my questions.

So, here she was. A rather inconspicuous, grey-haired American
lady of sixty-four, with a purse on her lap, sitting a little bent-over in
the lobby of the hotel and staring at the shop-windows on the other
side of the street with an expression on her face that you might come
across in a waiting-room, a kind of empty look. A round face, plump
hands and nose, and a somewhat pear-shaped double chin. Her eyes
I could not see from where I was standing.

I rushed into the elevator, really not sure whether or not I dared to
accost her, whether or not I wanted to interview her. From my room
I got the copy of the *Complete Poems* in which I had been saving my
questions for the past four years. With the questions was a poem
about her work I had once written and—at the time—translated into
English. Perhaps it was not translated quite correctly but still it was
better than stammering out: "I like your poems, I think you're one of
the best poets I have ever read," though it came to the same thing,
of course.

When I returned to the lobby she was talking with one of the
organizers of Poetry International. I sat down in an adjacent arm-
chair.

She had sharp, light blue eyes that gleamed off and on in a greenish shade. She was folding and unfolding her hands and seemed to be listening rather absent-mindedly to the bearded man. When he finally moved away, I shouted to myself "Go ahead, it's your turn. Let's go." And I went up to her.

The first thing she noticed was, not me, but the *Collected Poems* that I was holding. She expressed surprise that I owned the book and asked if she could hold it for a moment, to make a correction in it. "A stupid error," she said, while taking out her fountain-pen, putting on her spectacles, and changing, on page 177, "What nothing" into "But no." After that she asked, looking just over her glasses, if I would like her to sign the book. I would. She struck out her name on the title-page and wrote her signature above it in tiny, spidery handwriting.

I started to talk about the possibility of conducting an interview. She listened while putting her fountain-pen and spectacles back in her purse. "I hate interviews," she said. But in saying it she laughed for the first time, with a touch of such friendliness that I laughed back at her, mumbling "For sure." I told her how I had wanted to interview her before and waved my list of questions before her. She wanted to look at them beforehand. I then asked if I could phone her next day.

The next morning I saw her quite early in the hotel breakfast-room. She seemed somehow to have forgotten our non-committal arrangement. She had not yet had time for the questions. She asked would I telephone her at her room in an hour.

Killing time by turning the pages of her *Collected Poems,* I considered the joys and woes of the interviewer. Sixty-four. It was, after all, like interviewing one's own mother. In one way or another there was something indecent in it. I phoned at the appointed hour and we decided to meet at three in the hotel lobby.

It was a bit stupid to give away those questions, for of course I had not copied them.

At three I was present in the lobby, armed with her *Complete Poems* and my tape-recorder. I sat down and looked outside, just as she had done the day before. It became a quarter past three, half past three. A secret joy took possession of me. I had tried, but she hadn't shown up. Forevermore I would have almost interviewed Elizabeth Bishop. When I had totally accepted my situation and had ordered a beer in honor of it, she stepped out of a cab.

Only then did I see that she was rather heavy-set and had a mannish walk. She was wearing a blouse of an indeterminate light-brown color—tea with lots of milk—with a pattern of black, navy-blue, and peacock-blue stripes.

She smoothed out my little questionnaire on the table. I noticed that here and there she had scribbled things in the margin. "Let's see what I can answer on this." When I took out my tape-recorder, she shook her head, resolutely. "I hate tape-recorders. They make me nervous."

Okay, let's write. My first question was about her youth. Had the fact that she, early on an orphan, had been educated by grandparents, on both sides, influenced her work. The question had not been well formulated. It had read, "educated by elder people." She had written above it, "Isn't everyone?" I assent with "unfortunately, yes." She was a person who indeed didn't like interviews.

The second question was about painters. Elizabeth Bishop's work has often been compared with that of painters: her preference for minute description, her alertness to landscape, her search for the exact word-combinations to record subtle shades of color, her endless attention to detail.

She explained that she had just left the Boymans Museum, her reason for being late. She had stood admiringly in front of Bosch's paintings for a long time.

Were there painters who had influenced her work?

She looked at me as if I had asked whether there were any cabinet-makers who had had an influence on the development of her work.

Edward Hopper? I tried.

"The loneliness of the city. Yes, I know his work. I don't like it that much. I don't much like the city."

But he did paint many pictures of the coast north of Boston, I said.

"Some of them, yes.

"Those with lighthouses. Those are fine."

As if she were still thinking about my question, she answered suddenly: "An uncle of mine. Uncle George. My grandmother owned four of his paintings. He was a sailor, just like my great-grandfather, and by his twelfth year he was already painting and making ship-models. I wrote a new poem about this. It is called 'Poem' and has to do with one of his pictures. I had already written about him once before.''

"In 'Large Bad Picture,' you mean?''

"Yes.''

"Was he a good painter?''

"He was a very bad painter.''

"Poem" tells of a place, somewhere in Nova Scotia where Elizabeth spent a part of her childhood and which she recognizes via the picture. She too used to go there and, just like her uncle George, look at the grass, the sky, and the birds. The coinciding of two gazes that never regarded one another but looked on at the same scene, is the subject of the poem. She never knew her uncle George, but looking at his picture brought them together for a while. Later on she tells how she went back to the place where, as a girl, she spent a sailing holiday, and how she had been shocked that everything had changed. "That's one of the places I never want to go back to.''

Perhaps this is one of the motives of her writing: to make a record against change. She likes travelling and has traveled her whole life. Yet (or exactly for that reason) she is constantly at work, freezing all those movements in extraordinarily delicate still-lifes, in which everything is equally important and in which one can perceive her unwillingness to choose between the important and the not important. I quote her line: "Everything only connected by 'and' and 'and.' ''

"I don't know,'' she says. "Perhaps it is because I am none too well trained in philosophy. Some years ago somebody pointed to resemblances between my work and that of Wittgenstein.''

I raise my eyebrows, saying that I don't quite get that one.

"Neither do I, but that woman's father introduced Wittgenstein in America.'' For the first time the two of us laughed at the same time. Well, not laughing. Rather it was more like smiling benevolently, which sometimes ends up, just like her talking, in mid-sentence and passes into a looking around.

She tells of someone with whom she is friendly and who has written an essay about a mutual acquaintance.

"When I was talking to him about her splendid deep blue eyes, he looked at me in astonishment. He had never noticed them. And then this person remarks that it must be dreadful to pick up everything so precisely. On the contrary. It is marvelous. Of course he was writing just about himself."

I try to bring the conversation back to her poetry, to how her poems come about.

"Sometimes quickly, sometimes slowly. The shape depends on the 'items,' on the few lines with which the poem starts."

I observe that her poems seem to be rather distant, both literally and figuratively, showing, at first, little emotion.

"Emotion is essential. The only question is in what form. I am at work on a villanelle that is pure emotion."

"And what about your interest in maps, tapestries, images of reality?"

"The poem to which you refer, 'The Map,' had to do with a red map. There was nothing particularly noteworthy about it, but I was attracted by the way the names were running out from the land into the sea. As for that poem about a tapestry, that was inspired by an exhibit of medieval tapestries. And I like painting myself. Two years ago, in Chicago, there was an exhibit of authors who paint. Two of my pictures were exhibited there. I was very proud of it."

I ask about the style of her pictures.

"A bit naïve."

"Something like your uncle George?"

"Slightly better, perhaps."

Again and again I run up against a distinguished being who is not willing to talk about herself or her work. Yes, but that's the very reason for my sitting here.

"Your new collection, coming out in October, is called *Geography III*. Why?"

"I think of a remark of W. H. Auden in *Journal to a War,* which I am unable to quote, but which says, more or less, that if we could travel as fast as light, geography should be by far the most important thing to us."

"And that *III*?"

"I like threes."

"And travelling?"

"I like the sea and places on the seashore. We lived in Brazil for a number of years, some of them in the interior, but I am always looking for the coast."

The larger meaning of this "back-to-the-coast" remark is suggested by a hazy look. Poems are poems. It is up to the reader to give them sense.

"The other day I was considering that by and by I will have made all the journeys taken by my great-grandfather. Only in a more pleasant way, of course. Some time ago I took a sailing trip with friends, starting out from Mexico. Just off the coast there are heaps of little islands. On one of them were rows of white pelicans, all of them standing with their bills turned in the direction of the wind. It was quite funny. It reminded me of Edward Lear. Nowadays they winter on Cape Cod."

She has traveled a lot, but did live in Brazil for over twenty years. Why did she leave? Was it for political reasons?

"I haven't been back in two years. I had friends living there and they died. I still have a house there and it has still to be sold. Now I live in Boston, in a warehouse on the harbor. Soon I will return to see a parade of old windjammers that, on the occasion of the Bicentennial, will also visit Boston. That's what I want to see, sitting in front of my window. But first I leave here for Lisbon, to see friends. And to swim."

I ask her about poets who have influenced her work.

"George Herbert and Gerard Manley Hopkins. And Stevens for a while. That rarifying of his rather pleased me, but later on he became too abstract for me."

"And Marianne Moore? You wrote a poem about her."

"Marianne was one of my best friends. I knew her for quite a long time, a very special woman. In the beginning when I came to know her she didn't know I was writing. Later on she knew. But after Marianne and her mother 'rewrote' entirely one of my poems and made a parcel of it, sticking a gold star on it, I didn't let her read anything else. She seldom talked about anyone else's work. She used to work intensively on a poem, carrying it around on her clipboard, everywhere in the house—the bedroom, the kitchen. In the living room she had a big embroidery basket, filled with papers. Those papers were versions of one single poem. They were poor for a very long time. Her mother was a special woman, though somewhat odd. She was always trying to convert me, holding my hands while she prayed for the salvation of my soul. One day Marianne wrote a poem that was not about animals. I thought it very beautiful. The comment made by her mother, who had a very deep voice and spoke very slowly, was: 'Finally, for once you have left the zoo in peace.' During her last years Marianne was in a very bad way. Understanding her was difficult. And recall that I never knew another person to talk as much as she did. In her *Collected Poems* she spoiled some things, a great pity. For a while, now, I have been working on an essay about Marianne, but I just cannot bring it to conclusion. I must finish it.''

"Since 1970 you have been teaching at Harvard University. How do you like it?''

"To be honest about it, I started teaching too late. I have to read too much poetry, but there are some students who are doing well, who are publishing. So I really have to do it.''

Once more she goes through my list of questions. It is clear by now that she thinks we have had quite enough. About others she is more talkative than about herself, and that again squares with her poetry. She gets up and as she shakes my hand, says, "I'm glad you didn't ask about 'The Fish.' ''

"The Fish"—that's the poem by which she is represented in all the anthologies.

A Poet Who Doesn't Wear Her Woes

Leslie Hanscom / 1977

Reprinted from *Newsday*, 6 February 1977, Ideas, 8.

There is no real throne to which an American can aspire, but there
are seats of honor. One of them is a chair in the American Academy
of Arts and Letters, an elected group of 50 members who are admitted
to this avowedly restricted club for their conspicuous achievement.
The chair is no mere figure of speech; it is an actual place to sit—in a
courtlike room in an ornate building now marooned in the urban
jungle of Manhattan's Upper West Side.

A chair opens up only when the occupant dies and his or her name
is inscribed on the back along with the earlier holders (e.g. Frank
Lloyd Wright, William Dean Howells). With the death of Thornton
Wilder, a chair has opened up to Elizabeth Bishop. At 65, Miss
Bishop is our most honored American woman poet still living. She
has won the Pulitzer Prize and the National Book Award, and at the
beginning of this year, her new book of poems, *Geography III* (Farrar,
Straus, $7.95) was given the newest of the prestige prizes, the award
of the National Book Critics Circle.

Practically the only honor she hasn't won is popular recognition—if
that's an honor. The women poets who have most attracted public
interest in recent years have done so by wearing their woes on their
sleeves, which is not Elizabeth Bishop's way. The emotion of her
poetry is controlled, and her style is descriptive. She writes less about
herself than about what she sees—which is a lot. Her friend and
fellow poet, Robert Lowell, has written of her "humorous, command-
ing genius for picking up the unnoticed, now making something
sprightly and right, and now a great monument."

Elizabeth Bishop is a small, retiring woman with a pleasant, full-
fleshed face and gray hair. She lives in Boston, but the other day, on
a visit to New York, she was staying at the Cosmopolitan Club, where
the thick carpets made her reluctant, in the winter cold, to shake

hands for fear of electrical shock. For much of her life, she said, she had been used to warmer climes. From 1952 to 1968, she made her home in Brazil, and there is still a house there that she would like to sell.

The comment has been made that Brazil left its mark on Miss Bishop's poetry by contributing an element of tropical floridity to her native New England severity, but poetry had nothing to do with her reason for settling down there. She was touring South America, Miss Bishop recalled, when she stopped off in Brazil and almost immediately poisoned herself by sampling the cashew fruit. The cashew, it appears, is indeed a fruit, quite apart from the nuts which grow attached to it.

"I happen to be one of those Nordics," she said, "to whom it is poison. During the war, there were some American aviators stationed in northern Brazil, and it was discovered that one man in every 200 or so was allergic to the cashew." Violently ill from making her own discovery, Miss Bishop stayed on in Brazil to recover, made friends there and eventually wound up buying a home.

In the town of Petrópolis where she lived, some 50 miles from Rio, she became a local celebrity after winning the Pulitzer Prize in 1955. "They make a much bigger fuss there over that sort of thing," she said. "I was glad to win the prize because, up to that time, most people seemed to think I didn't do anything at all. Afterward, the man who used to sell me fruit said to a woman I knew, 'All my customers are so lucky. There is another lady who entered the lottery and won a bicycle.' That was fame in Petrópolis."

In her expatriate years, Miss Bishop wrote poems and short stories, edited an anthology of Brazilian poetry and translated into English *The Diary of Helena Morley,* the recollections of a girl growing up in a mining camp. Toward the end of the 1960s, she began to feel isolated in her foreign home and accepted an offer to return to the U.S. and teach. She now conducts two courses in verse-writing at Harvard.

Elizabeth Bishop has no illusions about the size of her audience. "Americans are embarrassed by poetry," she said, "it makes them nervous." Yet her classes are popular. "Oh, yes," she said, "there are still young people who want to write poetry. In the advanced class that I teach, I can only take 10 students, but 40 or 50 apply." What can aspiring poets be taught? "I think you can at least improve their

taste," she said, "and that's a service even if they are only going to
go on reading for the rest of their lives."

Her own beginnings as a poet go back to the age of eight. Miss
Bishop remembers a morning when her grandmother, preparing her
for Sunday school, was sprucing up her shoes. The shoes were patent
leather with white tops. To clean the tops, the grandmother used
gasoline, and Vaseline for the patent leather. The little girl was
intoxicated by the rhyme. "I went around all day chanting 'gasoline/
Vaseline,' " the older Elizabeth Bishop said. "It may not have been a
poem, but it was my first rhyme."

She still enjoys rhyme, makes irregular use of it and argues its
merits to her students, who think it an obsolete device. She used to
have similar discussions with her friend and mentor, Marianne Moore,
whose eminence among poets some believe she has inherited. "Marianne Moore used to say, 'Rhyme is dowdy,' but she wasn't consistent.
Sometimes she would call me on the telephone and ask me to help her
find a rhyme." Miss Bishop thinks her friend was an authentically
great poet, but she can't think of many others among women. She
even has mixed feelings about Emily Dickinson—not the courageous
eccentric who doggedly wrote poetry too original for its time without
hope of seeing it published, but the chronic complainer in verse. "I
am not attracted," she said, "by the oh-the-agony-of-it school."

David W. McCullough's Eye on Books

David W. McCullough / 1977

Reprinted from David W. McCullough, *People, Books and Book People* (New York: Harmony Books, 1981), 20–24.

When the Modern Language Association, during its convention last December, began a long session devoted to Elizabeth Bishop and her poetry, Miss Bishop ducked out and went around the corner to a delicatessen. Why? "For one thing," she said the other day, "I don't know how anyone can sit through one of those meetings. For another, the Stage serves the best corned beef hash in Manhattan."

In 1969, when she won the National Book Award for her prematurely titled *The Complete Poems,* she was in Brazil (she lived there for sixteen years) and word was brought to her by the police. "I came back from shopping and outside my door were two men in uniform, one with a lot of gold braid and the other wearing a tin helmet. They both snapped to attention and saluted me. It scared my little maid to death."

This year she won the National Book Critics Circle Award for her new collection of poems, *Geography III,* and she came down to New York from Boston to accept the prize. For many of the critics at the ceremony it was their first chance to see one of the legendary figures of modern American poetry, a woman whose poems are as open and accessible as she is shy and reticent.

"I've gone up and down the East Coast," she said when we met recently, "living everywhere from Nova Scotia to Key West, but I've never seemed to live long enough in one place to become a member of a poetry 'group,' and when I was in Brazil there weren't any groups handy. I've been a friend of Marianne Moore's and Robert Lowell's but not a part of any school."

She seems amused by the fact that both Moore and Lowell became compulsive tinkerers who often reworked their poems even after they were published. "All that revision never interested me," she says, "but Marianne Moore's greatest influence on me was a thirst for accuracy. She would go to incredible pains to get things right." For "Crusoe in England," in *Geography III,* Miss Bishop had a friend visit a goat farm to find out how goats open their eyes, and for "The Moose" she searched through maps in the Boston and Harvard libraries in search of the name of a particular Nova Scotia swamp. She finally came across it in a secondhand-book store in Bermuda, in the yellowing memoirs of a 19th-century missionary. But she doesn't carry factual accuracy to pedantic extremes. "In the Waiting Room" describes a *National Geographic* magazine she read in a dentist's office in 1918, the February issue. "Out of curiosity I looked it up, and it turned out that I had combined the March and February issues, but I didn't change the poem. It was right the way it was. I think Robert Lowell thinks I carry the accuracy business too far. When he gave me his new manuscript to read, he said, 'Oh, you'll just find mistakes.' "

The poem that the judges of the National Book Critics Circle picked out for special mention was "The Moose," which mixes the events of a bus trip from Nova Scotia to Boston with memories of childhood. "It is one of the few poems my Canadian relatives have liked," she says. Although she was born in Massachusetts, she spent her early years with her grandparents in Nova Scotia. "It was written in bits and pieces over a number of years and, finally, it all came together. After I read it in public for the first time, at Harvard, one of the students said, 'For a poem it wasn't bad.' "

One of the most moving poems in the book has for a refrain: "The art of losing isn't hard to master." It mentions three "loved houses." "Yes," she says, "one in Key West, one in Petrópolis, just west of Rio Bay, and one in Ouro Prêto, also in Brazil. The Ouro Prêto house was built in 1690, and from the front porch you can see seven baroque churches. I called it Casa Mariana, after Marianne Moore and because it was on the road to a town called Mariana. When I left I took the name plaque off the door. There are so many places I'll never go back to. I change, the places change. I was afraid to go back to Nova Scotia, but I went not long ago, and it hadn't changed."

Poetry Born Out of Suffering

Beatriz Schiller / 1977

Reprinted from *Jornal do Brasil* (Rio de Janeiro) (May 8, 1977), pp. 22–23.

"Poetess of the poets" and "the most refined talent in North-American literature," Elizabeth Bishop is famous for her elusiveness. Her telephone number is not in the book and at Harvard University, she is never in her office. She is nomadic, and with a vengeance. Traveling around the world, North to South, she landed in Brazil in 1951, brought there by virtue of one of the several fellowships she has received for her work. Her original plan was to voyage down the coast of South America to the Straits of Magellan. But in Rio, while visiting friends, including Lota de Macedo Soares whom she had met in 1942 in New York, she suffered a severe allergic reaction to "the juice from a cashew." She stayed on for medical treatment.

For 20 years, dating from the time of her allergic attack, she lived in Brazil. With her friend Lota she shared a house in Samambaia—which they built together—and an apartment in Rio. Later on she lived in Ouro Prêto, and to this day she owns a fully furnished house in that city. Several of her poems originated in Brazil. They describe our scenery, along with the human—and inhuman—characteristics that feature it. In contrast with many other foreigners, Elizabeth Bishop does not paint a Brazil that is exotic, but one that is intimately and deeply felt.

Her oeuvre is small, her poems short. But her prizes are many: a Pulitzer, for poetry (1956); an Ingram–Merrill award (1968); another from the American Academy of Arts and Letters (1960); a National Book Award (1968); the Order of the Baron of Rio Branco (1969); and, last year, the Neustadt International Prize for Literature/Books Abroad. The journal *World Literature Today* devoted 50 pages to Elizabeth Bishop, including literary criticism by Octávio Paz, John Ashbery, and other literary experts.

Meanwhile, Elizabeth continues in her routine. At 65 she is once again living in Massachusetts, where she was born. She lives in an old building, a warehouse on the docks converted into residences. She teaches two courses at Harvard, one on prose, the other on poetry. Among her unpublished work, there is a collection of small prose pieces on Brazil, telling of her trips—one of them with Aldous Huxley, as far as Amazonas—and speaking of her responses to Brazilian music and architecture. Some (a few) of her poems have been translated into Portuguese. Many of them have been rendered into Spanish, Russian, French, Italian, Arabic, Japanese and Danish.

Beyond spreading news of her "poetic" Brazil throughout the world, Elizabeth Bishop has also brought a bit of our literature and art to the United States. Working with Emanuel Brasil, she has compiled *An Anthology of Twentieth-Century Brazilian Poetry* that runs from Manuel Bandeira to Ferreira Gullar. She has translated Helena Morley's *Minha Vida de Menina* and Henrique Mindlin's *Arquitectura Moderna Brasileira*. Currently, once again with Emanuel Brasil, she is preparing a second anthology of Brazilian poetry, ranging from Ferreira Gullar to our youngest poets, with whom she has kept up-to-date.

"My father died when I was eight months old. When I was four years old my mother went mad. I was left alone. My mother's sister, a married aunt with no children, took care of me. Afterwards I was sent to a private school, and later I went off to the university."

In 1930 Elizabeth Bishop took her degree at Vassar College, an aristocratic school. In a week she had become accustomed to the residential college, though she continued to feel very much alone. On vacations she went to a girls' camp on Cape Cod, to sail. From childhood on she has suffered from allergies, asthma, and migraine. During her entire life periods of relative health have been followed by long stays in hospitals.

"At this very moment I am not feeling well. I have had to take cortisone for an allergy and feel swollen."

It is apparent that Elizabeth has become accustomed to suffering but has not allowed it to turn into hatred for the world, as it has with some people. Her poetry is indisputably buoyant, hopeful.

"I am really optimistic. At least on the surface. Once a year I get depressed, but that doesn't last long. I do find that the Brazilians are very much given to depression. They are very temperamental."

And what is the secret that keeps her from being sad?

"I find that over time people stabilize. Yet even that is not entirely true. Just this week I became greatly depressed. My physician visited me and brought over my whole medical history, my entire life since I was a little girl. It was too much for me. But I did not want to let my sadness show, and we did have a good time. We went out walking. And of course, teaching as I am now doing, I have to keep up a happy front. See, the Americans from New England are great hypocrites. It's part of tradition not to show one's feelings. But sometimes I show mine."

Her poetry is precise. Everything gets said in a few words and with great intensity. But she doesn't like to talk about her work. She prefers to generalize.

"The poets of my generation have a great freedom of choice. They can rhyme or not. I use what seems to work best, without its having anything to do with subject matter. At times I change horses in mid-stream. I begin a poem, but years later I see that I do not like it the way it was written. What started out being one poem frequently turns into another one."

Elizabeth is the enemy of formulas and schemes.

"Some poets feel a need to use more tricks to express themselves than I do. Perhaps it is because they try to express something from the inside out—from—what shall I call them—their souls. Not I. I am more impersonal. I always have been. It is true that some people call me cold. I don't agree. But no doubt, I am different from those who like confessional poetry."

Elizabeth Bishop writes geographically—*North & South—A Cold Spring, Questions of Travel, Complete Poems* and *Geography III* are some of her books. And in all of them the external environment predominates over the interior universe.

"I think that that nonsense of confessional poetry started with Robert Lowell. But the vogue is dying out. And Lowell, after all, was talking about his family. He was not historically emotional, as were so many who came later."

And what of the new poets? What are the tendencies today in American poetry?

"There are so many people in this country. Diversity is an American characteristic. There is much happening, undoubtedly. I would say that one thing of great importance is the quantity of translations, which open our eyes to foreign cultures. There are two or three great projects going on, one at Columbia University and another at the University of Texas, for example, in which great sums are being invested in the translation of poetry and prose. Brazilian literature is becoming better known here, and I believe that I might deserve some of the credit for spreading the word. An *Anthology of Twentieth-Century Brazilian Poetry* is in its fourth printing. Mark Strand, another poet, has just translated a book by Manuel Bandeira. As for myself, I translate a poem only when I feel that it can work in English, when I can preserve its meter and rhythm.''

In some of her poems about Brazil there are expressions taken, indisputably, from the Portuguese. In "Arrival in Santos" ("Chegada a Santos"), she says, after describing the port: "We leave Santos at once. / We are traveling to the interior." ("Viajando para o interior" is common Portuguese. In English, and especially for Elizabeth Bishop, who always lived near the sea, it takes on the different meaning of a journey into the self, as well as into the country.) That phrase has been quoted by many critics. Why did she employ it? Elizabeth smiles, and says:

"Because it was a good rhyme. I did not speak Portuguese though I understood the language a little, thanks to the Spanish I learned in Mexico. It was impossible to learn Portuguese with my Brazilian friends, since they all spoke excellent English. I began to understand the language itself in the kitchen."

Elizabeth Bishop offers me an espresso. For a moment I feel as if I were back in Brazil. I see Brazilian furniture and objects, engravings in wood, ornaments, a large "figa" hanging on the door. There are many books in bookcases and on tables, books about ships, seashells, and animals.

"I am not a verbal person, I do not know how to talk very well. I am an observer, and one of the things I like to observe is nature. I love zoology. I should tell you that I do not like to talk about literature, except when resolving a specific problem."

Conversation remains difficult, and for a moment it is like pulling teeth. Elizabeth does not search for pretty phrases nor does she set out to propose theories.

"Portuguese did not influence my choice of words. Latin, yes. I also studied Greek. I like words very much and I love dictionaries.

My dream is to have a complete *Webster,* in 13 volumes. But it costs so much."

Elizabeth took a boat up the Rio São Francisco in 1966. On the trip she kept a diary.

"I love uneventful journeys. Eight days on the boat, going as far as possible. The Rio São Francisco is disappearing because they are using all the waterfalls for hydroelectric power. Already there are fewer boats, and water is becoming scarce."

She travelled to Bahia and the Amazonas. And she returned to the hills of the state of Rio.

"I like the country. I loved living in Petrópolis. An ideal place. Sometimes we'd get a bit bored and go off to Rio. Not that Rio at that time had that much to offer in the way of cinema or shopping. I also liked going to Cabo Frio, where we used to spend Christmas."

In Elizabeth Bishop's poetry it is still possible to catch a glimpse of a Brazil that is disappearing: "The sad, two-noted, wooden tune/ of disparate wooden clogs/ carelessly clacking over/ a grease-stained filling-station floor" ("Questions of Travel"). In "Song for the Rainy Season," she sings of Samambaia, the oasis of an era that would come to an end: "rejoice! For a later era will differ." The truth is that long ago, when a child, she learned that life was fragile.

Elizabeth Bishop was living in Petrópolis when she received the Pulitzer Prize for poetry.

"I'm going to tell you a most amusing story. The news came in the papers, which was a very good thing because some of my Brazilian friends doubted that I was truly a poet. After all, if I did know how to write poetry, why was I in Brazil? I find that the Brazilians believe much more in prizes than do the Americans. Well, on that occasion there appeared in a Rio newspaper several photographs—horrible ones, by the way. My friend Lota went shopping at the green grocer's. He asked her: 'That girl in the newspaper, isn't she Dona Elizabeth?' My friend explained that it was so and that I had won a poetry prize. The vegetable man smacked his lips and wagged his head: 'Isn't that fantastic! All my customers are very lucky. She's the second one. Last week, Dona So-and-So bought a raffle ticket and won a bicycle!' I love this story, it's marvelous."

Had life in Brazil, less harried at the time, given her the tranquillity that she could not have had in the United States?

"I was able to work in Brazil because I had no distractions. For the first time in my life I had a study of my own, one that was peaceful, holding all my books, in the middle of a grove. Only on weekends did we have visitors."

"As a child I often went to Samambaia," I tell her. "I remember entering your house, on tiptoe, and overhearing my neighborhood friends saying: 'Two strange women live here; they never leave the house.' "

"That's not true. It's a child's exaggeration. We didn't go to parties every night, but neither were we hermits. We had plenty of friends. Some of them, like Carlos Lacerda, were neighbors in the same part of town. Other friends came from greater distances. Manuel Bandeira used to come up to sample tidbits. He had a weakness for sweets. He even wrote me a poem, the only one he ever wrote in English: 'I wish I had two bellies/ because of your good jellies.' He told me that those two lines were so good that he could think of nothing that could follow them."

Roberto Burle-Marx, Aldous Huxley, Marianne Moore, Robert Lowell, John Dewey, Ezra Pound, Octávio Paz were her friends. But now her friends are few, most of them having died.

"Today I have only a single great friend, one whose parents were also my friends. Ricardo Xavier Lobo Sternberg, 27 years old, who graduated from Berkeley, writes in Portuguese, and above all, in English. He is just emerging as a poet. He studies at Harvard and we see each other all the time. In May we are going to do a program at a school near New Bedford, where the population is nearly all Portuguese. Ricardo plays the guitar. We are going to read and sing Brazilian poetry, in the original and in English translation."

"And which Brazilian poets do you favor?"

"I find Brazilian poetry marvelous, much better, actually, than the prose, in my opinion. I very much like Carlos Drummond de Andrade and João Cabral de Melo Neto. But in saying that I am not saying that I do not like the others. There are many talented poets in Brazil. I have heard that the latest generation has been influenced by the Americans, but in general Brazilians are greatly influenced by the French. I do not like to generalize, however. I cannot speak of 'a Brazilian way of thinking' because the 'carioca's' mentality is totally different from the 'paulista's' or 'mineiro's.' "

"What is your general impression of Brazil?"

"I have no theories about Brazil, unlike so many people. Immediately upon arriving I did have theories and they were sharp ones. Little by little those theories evaporated. Brazil became my home."

"And how about the house in Petrópolis?"

"I do not want to see our house in Petrópolis. Never again. I also want to sell my house in Ouro Prêto. I started out here, in Boston, and it is natural that I end up here."

Lota de Macedo Soares died. The cat "Tobias" also died. Elizabeth accepted a teaching job at Harvard.

"It wasn't the political changes in Brazil that caused me to leave. It was simply the fact that I had accepted a job. For many years I had the pleasure of being the only American poet who did not have to teach classes. I had some money when I went to Brazil and living was less expensive, a situation that changed, however. I was awarded many fellowships. Whenever I feared that I was about to end up in the poorhouse, something would happen. I was very pleased to be invited to teach at Harvard, but next year I must stop. I am too old to teach, I am 65. I could continue if I had tenure, but I do not have the degrees required for that. But I have already been invited elsewhere. I am going to give courses at New York University. I shall take the shuttle twice a week."

"How did you prepare for a life of poetry?"

"I studied music, afterwards changing over to English literature. Literature, Latin, Greek, Zoology. I don't know which subject helped me the most. I never took courses on how to write. Actually, in my time they did not exist. They are a new thing. I tell my students that instead of learning to write poetry, they would do better to study Latin and Greek. Hardly any of them have studied Latin. In the past Latin was mandatory. I find that while it is not essential, having Latin sharpens one's control over other languages. The universities should teach things that can be taught. I find it nonsensical to go to the university to learn to be creative."

Yet at the moment there are courses in creativity in the United States, beginning with kindergarten and right up to graduate school.

"I am totally against it. I think that students should learn things like languages, science, and even, to a certain point, literature. These are the tools they will work with later. Though I shouldn't say all this because the courses I teach are my bread and butter."

"How do you teach your classes in poetry?"

"It is very difficult. Classes are small, ten students. To be admitted to the class they must present their poems. I read them and I try to imagine who are the most intelligent ones. It is impossible to calculate that. It's horrible. But during the last semester I had a very good group. And I am very hard. I give out "C's." Some of the other teachers don't do that, but I do. Every week I give them a list of things they must turn in. Sometimes I suggest a subject, other times a poetic form. Or I ask them to change one of today's poems into an 'old' one."

"How is it that one chooses to study poetry, to become a poet?"

"The majority do not want to be poets, but they do want to have some control over that form of expression. I have an Irish student who has a talent for comic verse. He wrote three plays in a year. He will probably go in for musical comedy. In my seven years of teaching, I have had three truly talented students, poets—which is marvelous, a good proportion. One of them has already published a couple of poems. I have another excellent student who certainly could publish a book."

Being against labels and simplifications, Elizabeth Bishop also does not like judging a poet by the whole of his work.

"Some poets, perhaps because they are more competitive, want to rate everything numerically. Students also tend to do this. I discourage the practice. It is better to discard that which is bad and to save one's interest for what is good in each poet, than pitting them against each other."

A Conversation with Elizabeth Bishop

George Starbuck / 1977

Copyright © 1977, by George Starbuck, published in *Plough-shares,* vol. 3, nos. 3 and 4 (1977), 11–29.

A gray late afternoon in winter. Elizabeth Bishop, dressed casually in a Harvard jersey, welcomes the interviewer and answers his polite questions about a gorgeous gilt mirror on her livingroom wall. Yes, it is Venetian, those little blackamoors are Venetian, but it was picked up at an auction in Rio de Janeiro. The interviewer, sure in advance this is nothing to have asked one of his favorite poets to do, squares away with his cassette recorder on the coffee table and pops a prepared question. A wonderful expanse of books fills the wall behind the sofa. Before long there is laughter. A good memory, the thought of a quirk or extravagance in someone she knows and likes, sets Miss Bishop off. The laughter is quick, sharp, deep. No way to transcribe it.

GS: I did some research. I got out the travel book you wrote on commission for Time-Life Books. There's geography, too. You tell such wonderful bright clear stories from the history of Brazil.

EB: I can't remember too much of that book; rather, I choose not to. It was edited by Time-Life Books and they changed a lot of it. I wanted to use different, and more, pictures. There's one—the one of Dom Pedro [the last Emperor] and his official party taken in front of Niagara Falls? Well, there were more of that trip. But that one, I think, is really ironic. He travelled quite a bit in this country. And yet in Brazil he had never been to the Falls of Iguaçu, which are—how much—ten times bigger than Niagara Falls. . . . This was in 1876 and he went to the Philadelphia Centennial. Alexander Bell was there, with his telephone—a very young man, whose invention hadn't been used at all then. And Dom Pedro ordered telephones for his summer Palace, in Petrópolis. He also thought that the ladies of his court didn't have enough to do, so he took each of them back a Singer sewing machine—which they didn't like very much. Did you read in that Brazil book how Longfellow gave a dinner party for him, in Cambridge?

GS: Yes, and that Dom Pedro was fond of Whittier and translated some of his poems into Portuguese.

EB: I looked up those translations. I thought they would be Whittier's abolitionist poems, because Dom Pedro was very much against slavery. [Slavery existed in Brazil until 1888.] But they weren't those poems at all. They were poems about birds, nature poems.

Whittier was very shy and at the Longfellow dinner party Dom Pedro, who was over six feet tall, strong and handsome, tried to give him the Brazilian *abraço,* twice—and poor Whittier was frightened to death.

GS: You take a set task, like that Time-Life book, and make it wholly your own. [EB: Not wholly; say two-thirds.] It always seemed that you were bursting to tell those stories. You're that way with translations. I discovered something. I went into *Geography III* without stopping off at the Table of Contents, and so I went into the Joseph Cornell poem without realizing it was a translation from Octavio Paz.

EB: It's a wonderful poem in Spanish.

GS: And in English! That's what I thought: I was reading *your* poem about Cornell. Paul Carroll has a beautiful poem about Cornell's "Medici Slot Machine." And here I'm thinking, "Elizabeth Bishop has done an even better poem about Cornell," and I turn the last page and see it's a translation.

EB: Well, I thought, of course, I should put Octavio Paz's name at the beginning, and I had it that way at first, but it didn't look right. There was the title, and then the dedication line, and the author's name seemed like too many things under the title, so I decided to put it at the end.

GS: Well, you do good poems about paintings and such. The one in *Geography III* about noticing a little painting that has been looked at but not noticed much before . . .

EB: In my first book there is a poem called "Large Bad Picture"; that picture was by the same great-uncle, painted when he was about 14 years old. They were a very poor family in Nova Scotia, and he went to sea as a cabin boy. Then he painted three or four big paintings, memories of the far North, Belle Isle, etc. I loved them. They're not very good as painting. An aunt owned several of them. I tried to get her to sell them to me, but she never would. Then Great-Uncle George went to England, and he did become a fairly well-known "traditional" painter. In 1905, I think it was, he went back to Nova Scotia for the summer to visit his sister, my grandmother. He made a lot of sketches and held "art classes" for my aunts and my mother and others. I eventually fell heir to this little sketch ("About the size of an old-style dollar bill"), the one I describe. Helen Vendler has written a wonderful paper in which she talks about this poem. Do you use this tape machine to record music, readings, things like that?

GS: This is only the second time I've used it for anything.

EB: I tried doing a lot of letters in Brazil on tape, but I gave up.

GS: I've even heard of people trying to write on them. Richard Howard trained himself to translate using a tape recorder. He was doing DeGaulle's memoirs and all those *nouveaux romans*. Book after book, for a living. He says he disciplined himself to do the whole job in two, or at most three, headlong runs through, reading the French and talking the English into the tape, having a typist transcribe it, running through again.

EB: I didn't know that was the way he did it. What was it, a hundred and twenty-seven novels? I translated *one* fairly long Brazilian book, a young girl's diary. It's probably full of mistakes, because it was one of the very first things I did. I had just started reading, trying to learn Portuguese. Someone suggested it, and I began. It was painful. I began writing in a big notebook, but a third of the way through I finally caught on to the child's style or thought I did. Then I began to translate directly on the typewriter, the rest of it. It took me about three years, as it was. Some people can write poetry right off on a typewriter, I think. Dr. Williams did, I'm told.

GS: Some poets write it out so easily it scares you. We have a neighbor who was a very young nurse working in Boston, at Mass. General Hospital, maybe forty years ago. She told me the story one time, asking me if I'd ever heard of this strange person she worked for. A weird doctor there used to give her poems that he had scribbled on the back of prescription forms, toilet paper, anything, and ask her to type them up. She'd have to go sit on the stool in a small toilet off the hall, the only place she could be out of the way, and with the typewriter on her knees she'd type the things.

EB: Was it—?

GS: Yep, it was Merrill Moore. And he also used to dictate sonnets into a dictaphone while he was driving. I mean he had a hundred thousand sonnets to get written. Wasn't that the total finally?

EB: Did she like the poems, the sonnets, when she got them?

GS: She didn't know. She didn't presume.

I don't know how you could rush onto tape in translating poems. There's one in which you seem to have discovered something Brazilian that comes out perfectly in early English ballad style. The "Brothers of Souls! Brothers of Souls!" poem.

EB: Oh, yes. That "Severino" poem is only a few parts of a very long Christmas play. I saw it given. I've never done very much translation, and I've almost never done any to order, but every once in a while something seems to go into English. There's one poem in that book, "Travelling in the Family" (Carlos Drummond de Andrade) that came out very well, I think. The meter is almost exactly the same. Nothing had to be changed. Even the word order. Of course word order will naturally have to come out different, but this one happened to come out well. I wrote and asked Dr. Drummond if I could repeat one word instead of writing the line the way he had it, and he wrote back yes that would be fine. Portuguese has a very different metrical system, very like the French. But every once in a while a poem does go into English.

GS: I'm curious about one of your own that seems to go so easily. "The Moose."

EB: I started that, I hate to say how many years ago, probably twenty. I had the beginning, the incident with the moose, it really happened; and the very end; and the poem just sat around.

GS: Did that partial version of it have the other major movement or topic in it: the dreamy conversation, leading you back to the pillow-talk of grandparents?

EB: Yes. Yes, I'd always had that. I had written it down in notes about the trip. I'm sure it's happened to you, in planes or trains or buses. You know, you're very tired, half-asleep, half-awake. I think probably in this case it was because they were all speaking in Nova Scotian accents, strange but still familiar, although I couldn't quite make out much of what anyone was saying. But the Moose: that happens. A friend wrote me about an encounter like that, with a buck deer. He did exactly the same thing, sniffed the car all over. But in that case, instead of disappearing the way the moose did, he chased the car for about a mile.

GS: You obviously do like to know and use exact geographer's knowledge about things. You've got the language down pat, and the knowledge of particular things, but let me embarrass you: I admire the philosophy of the poems, the morals.

EB: I didn't know there were any . . .

GS: OK, OK. But the aubade that ends the book—"Five Flights Up." The way the "ponderousness" of a morning becomes, lightly, our ancient uninnocence: the depression of having a past and the knowledge of what's recurring: "Yesterday brought to today so lightly! / (A yesterday I find almost impossible to lift.)"

EB: Yes, quite a few people seemed to like that poem . . .

GS: I'm a sucker for that.

EB: It must be an experience that everybody's had. You know, about my first book one fairly admiring friend wound up by saying, "But you have no philosophy whatever." And people who are really city people are sometimes bothered by all the "nature" in my poems.

GS: I suppose Crusoe was a city kid. It's such fun, the accuracy with which you borrow flora and fauna for his little island ("Crusoe in England," in *Geography III*).

EB: It's a mixture of several islands.

GS: And the deliberate anachronisms too—like the Wordsworth reference.

EB: The *New Yorker* sent the proof back and beside that line was the word "anachronism," and also at another place in the poem, I think. But I told them it was on purpose. But the snail shells, the blue snail shells, are true.

GS: Are there snails like that on—what was his island—Juan Fernandez?

EB: Perhaps—but the ones I've seen were in the Ten Thousand islands in Florida. Years ago I went on a canoe trip there and saw the blue snails. They were tree snails, and I still may have some. They were very frail and broke easily and they were all over everything. Fantastic.

GS: He's an Adam there and you have this wonderful little penny-

ante Eden with "one kind of everything:/one tree snail . . . one variety
of tree . . . one kind of berry."

EB: The waterspouts came from Florida. We used to see them. You
know, I am inaccurate, though. And I get caught. The poem about
being almost seven, in the dentist's office, reading the *National
Geographic*?

GS: "You are an I,/you are an *Elizabeth,*/you are one of *them.*"

EB: Yes, that one. Something's wrong about that poem and I
thought perhaps that no one would ever know. But of course they find
out everything. My memory had confused two 1918 issues of the
Geographic. Not having seen them since then, I checked it out in the
New York Public Library. In the February issue there was an article,
"The Valley of 10,000 Smokes," about Alaska that I'd remembered,
too. But the African things, it turned out, were in the *next* issue, in
March. When I sent the poem to the *New Yorker* I wrote Howard
Moss and said I must confess that this is a little wrong. The magazine
was nice about it and said it would be all right. But, since then, two
people have discovered that it isn't right. They went and looked it up!
I should have had a footnote.

GS: Well, all the critics are poets and all the poets are critics, but if
there's a difference I believe in, it's that, as personalities, critics tend
to be more focused on mere literature. And so compendious Richard
Ellmann can do that big fat anthology, loaded with literary information
but when he has to footnote a place name, he puts the Galapagos
Islands in the Caribbean.

EB: He did it to me. I say "entering the Narrows of St. Johns" and
he has a footnote saying that's an island in the Caribbean, when it's
St. John's, Newfoundland.

GS: Poets are really seriously interested in places, in travels, in
discoveries about the world. . . . I've been rereading Lowes and
there's nothing at all stupid about that book, but he pretends Coleridge
had utterly unaccountable, just out-and-out screwball taste in light
reading. Travel tales! One of Lowes' tropes is to astonish the reader
with what Coleridge got from this obviously frivolous miscellaneous
grubbing around in things that nobody in his right mind would read.

EB: Yes.

GS: It serves his point, but here was an age when actual marvels were being discovered. Coleridge went after those books for the best possible reasons.

EB: And how do they know? It takes probably hundreds of things coming together at the right moment to make a poem and no one can ever really separate them out and say this did this, that did that.

GS: What got the Crusoe poem started?

EB: I don't know. I reread the book and discovered how really awful *Robinson Crusoe* was, which I hadn't realized. I hadn't read it in a long time. And then I was remembering a visit to Aruba—long before it was a developed "resort." I took a trip across the island and it's true that there are small volcanoes all over the place.

GS: I forget the end of *Robinson Crusoe*. Does the poem converge on the book?

EB: No. I've forgotten the facts, there, exactly. I reread it all one night. And I had forgotten it was so moral. All that Christianity. So I think I wanted to re-see it with all that left out.

GS: When you were very young, which were the poets you started with?

EB: When I went to summer camp when I was twelve, someone gave me an anthology—one of the first Harriet Monroe anthologies. That made a great impression. I'd never read any of those poets before. I had read Emily Dickinson, but an early edition, and I didn't like it much. And my aunt had books like Browning, Mrs. Browning, Tennyson, Ingoldsby's Legends . . .

GS: But later, when did you begin looking around and say to yourself "Who, among the poets in the generation ahead of me, are poets I'm going to have to come to terms with?"

EB: I don't think I ever thought of it that way, but perhaps that was Auden. All through my college years, Auden was publishing his early books, and I and my friends, a few of us, were very much interested in him. His first books made a tremendous impression on me.

GS: I don't see Auden rife in your earlier poems. In fact it struck me that the closest I had seen you come to an early Auden manner or materials was a recent poem, in the new book: "12 O'Clock News."

EB: Yes, that's recent. I think I tried not to write like him then, because everybody did.

GS: It's as if, all of a sudden, decades later, there's "On the Frontier"—something you could use in it.

EB: Actually that poem, "12 O'Clock News," was another that had begun years earlier. In a different version. With rhymes, I think. Yes, I got stuck with it and finally gave up. It had nothing to do with Viet Nam or any particular war when I first wrote it, it was just fantasy. This is the way things catch up with you. I have an early poem, a long poem, written a long time ago. The Second World War was going on, and it's about that, more or less. "Roosters," I wrote it in Florida, most of it. Some friends asked me to read it a year or so ago, and I suddenly realized it sounded like a feminist tract, which it wasn't meant to sound like at all to begin with. So you never know how things are going to get changed around for you by the times.

GS: But that makes some sense. Let's see, if I can find it in the book—Sure:

> where in the blue blur
> their rustling wives admire,
> the roosters brace their cruel feet and glare
>
> with stupid eyes
> while from their beaks there rise
> the uncontrolled, traditional cries.

I'm afraid it's their banner now. You'll never get it away from them. By the way, I've heard your "Filling Station" poem used as a feminist tract.

EB: Really?

GS: In a nice apt way, by Mona Van Duyn. She read, at Bread Loaf, in lieu of a lecture, one poem each by about eight American women, with a few words in between the poems. There were a couple of poems which she seemed to want to demonstrate were too tract-y to be of any use. A Robin Morgan poem . . .

EB: Oh heavens, yes.

GS: In that context, yours did seem a nice wry study of the "woman's touch."

EB: But no woman appears in it at all.

GS: But the pot, the flowers, the ...

EB: Crocheted doily, yes.

GS: The woman who is "not there," she's certainly an essential subject of the poem.

EB: I never saw the woman, actually. We knew the men there . . .

GS: But the evidence is . . .

EB: I never . . . Isn't it strange? I certainly didn't feel sorry for whoever crocheted that thing! Isn't that strange?

GS: Well, which are your feminist tracts?

EB: I don't think there are any. The first part of "Roosters," now, I suppose. But I hadn't thought of it that way. Tract poetry . . .

GS: What about back in college . . .

EB: I was in college in the days—it was the Depression, the end of the Depression—when a great many people were communist, or would-be communist. But I'm just naturally perverse, so I stood up for T. S. Eliot then. I never gave feminism much thought, until . . .

GS: You started to name poets important to you with a man, Auden. Did . . .

EB: When I was given that anthology when I was twelve or thirteen, in the introduction to it, Harriet Monroe, I suppose it was, talked about Hopkins, and quoted an incomplete fragment of a poem— "tattered-tasseled-tangled," and so on. I was immensely struck by those lines, and then when I went to school, in 1927 or 1928, the second Bridges edition of Hopkins came out and a friend gave me that. I wrote some very bad imitation Hopkins for a time, all later destroyed—or so I hope.

GS: Did it seem important to notice what women poets were doing?

EB: No, I never made any distinction; I never make any distinction. However, one thing I should make clear. When I was in college and started publishing, even then, and in the following few years, there were women's anthologies, and all-women issues of magazines, but I always refused to be in them. I didn't think about it very seriously, but I felt it was a lot of nonsense, separating the sexes. I suppose this feeling came from feminist principles, perhaps stronger than I was aware of.

GS: I had seen the sexist thing going on when I was a teacher in a poetry class where there happened to be some good young women poets who were, yes, exploring, systematically, trying to find positions for themselves or placements for themselves as women poets. Adrienne Rich said she had gotten to the point where she just didn't want to waste the time, in amenities and dues-paying and awkwardness, that it took, she felt, in a mixed class of male and female students . . .

EB: Really?

GS: Yes. To allow the women, of whom she obviously felt protective, to begin to talk openly and be fully and aggressively participating.

EB: I've never felt any sexual warfare in classes. Almost never.
Only once or twice, perhaps, and with one boy. Maybe I'm blind. Or
maybe my classes are too formal. The students are almost always
polite, even gentle, with each other; they seem to treat each other as
friends and equals . . . they don't argue much. The past two terms
I've had outstandingly good classes. I had a "party" for one class
here the night before last and I think we all had a good time. I've
never visited other people's workshops. Perhaps I should go and see
what they're like.

GS: Do you approve of all the creative writing classes . . .

EB: No. I try to discourage them! I tell students they'd be better
off studying Latin. Latin or Greek. They are useful for verse writing.
I have a feeling that if there is a great poet at Boston University or
Harvard now, he or she may be hiding somewhere, writing poetry
and not going to writing classes at all. However, I have had some
students who have done very well (two or three "geniuses" I think
and several very talented). I think the best one hopes for is that after
students graduate they'll continue to read poetry for the rest of their
lives. What can you teach, really teach? I'm a fussbudget, probably a
fiend. I give assignments. I find it hard not to rewrite poems or prose.
I try hard not to say "This is what you should do," but sometimes I
can't resist.

GS: What happens then?

EB: Well, sometimes they agree with me—often they meekly agree
with me!

GS: Why does that seem so dangerous and almost forbidden to do?
I know it does and I agree with you. But look at painters. I was
shocked the first time I went to an art class and saw the professor
walking around picking up a brush, a palette knife.

EB: Just to change lines?

GS: Yes. There was this stuff on the student's easels and he
changed it.

EB: One student some years ago wanted badly to write. He was
very bright, but didn't show too much talent. I gave assignments,
very strict. When we read the results out loud, trying to be kind, I

said "Well, after all I don't expect you to do brilliantly on this; it's just a rather impossible assignment." He grew angry and said "You shouldn't say that! Any assignment isn't just an assignment, it's a poem!" Well, now I think he was right and I was wrong.

Again, about "feminism" or Women's Lib. I think my friends, my generation, were at women's colleges mostly (and we weren't all writers). One gets so used, very young, to being "put down" that if you have normal intelligence and have any sense of humor you very early develop a tough, ironic attitude. You just try to get so you don't even notice being "put down."

Most of my writing life I've been lucky about reviews. But at the very end they often say "The best poetry by a woman in this decade, or year, or month." Well, what's that worth? You know? But you get used to it, even expect it, and are amused by it. One thing I do think is that there are undoubtedly going to be more good women poets. I've been reading Virginia Woolf's letters. Have you read them?

GS: No. I've been reading a collection of Marianne Moore letters.

EB: Oh?

GS: Published by the University of Rochester Libraries.

EB: Oh, I have that. Anthony Hecht sent it to me. But those aren't such good letters. I mean, of course, they're fascinating. The woman she wrote them to, Hildegarde Watson, who died recently, was probably her best friend. But most of them have to do with clothes, and chitchat like that. I have quite a few of her letters, and some of them, especially the gossipy, personal, literary ones, are wonderful. Telling stories, quoting things, describing. It's very interesting, that little book, but I'm sure she wrote better letters than these.

GS: And you've been reading Woolf's?

EB: I'm reading Volume Two. And this is much more interesting. The first volume I thought was rather boring, but this is where she and Woolf start the Hogarth Press. And you see how she ran into prejudice. She doesn't complain about it much, but you sense it. When she wrote *Three Guineas,* her first "feminist" book, she was rather badly treated.

Many times she'll say how unhappy she is about reviews, . . . You know she could get very cross. Have you ever read *Three Guineas*? A wonderful little book. I think I have it here. (I need a librarian.)

This section down here should be Geography and Travel, and . . . Oh
here's Woolf. But not *Three Guineas*.

I haven't had one of these things for years. [Christmas candy canes
on the coffee table.] Peppermint sticks. You know what we used to
do, with peppermint sticks? You stick it in half a lemon, and you suck
the lemon juice through it.

I think I've been, oh, half-asleep all my life. I started out to study
music, to be a music major. And somehow, I got into trouble with
that. I liked it; I gave it up; I wasted a great deal of time; I studied
Greek for a while; well I wasn't very good at that; then, when I got
out of college, I thought I'd study medicine. At that time, I would
have had to take an extra year of chemistry and study German. I'd
already given up on German once. I actually applied to Cornell
Medical College. But I'd already published a few things, and friends—
partly Marianne Moore—discouraged me. Not just discouraged me.

GS: Had you submitted things to *The Dial,* or . . .

EB: *The Dial* had ceased to exist. There were other magazines . . .

GS: Well, how had Miss Moore found out about you in order to
discourage you from going into medicine?

EB: Oh. Well, I knew her. I've written a piece about this that I hope
to finish soon: how I happened to meet her through the librarian in
college. I had just read her poems in magazines and a few pieces in
anthologies. The mother of a friend of mine had first told me about
her, I think. But *Observations* wasn't in the Vassar Library.

I asked the librarian why she didn't have *Observations* in the
library. She said "Are you interested in her poetry?" (She spoke so
softly you could barely hear her.) And I said "Yes, very much." And
she said, "I've known her since she was a small child. Would you like
to meet her?" Imagine! It was the only time in my life that I've ever
attempted to meet someone I admired. The librarian had her own
copy of *Observations,* and lent it to me, but she obviously didn't think
much of it, because she'd never ordered a copy for the Vassar
Library. There were a lot of clippings—mostly unfavorable reviews—
tucked into it. And then I went to New York and met Miss Moore,
and discovered later that there had been other Vassar girls sent down
over the years, and that Miss Moore didn't look forward to this a bit.
But somehow we got along. She met me on the right-hand bench
outside the Reading Room at the N.Y. Public Library. A safe place to

meet people, since she could get rid of them quickly. But something worked—a stroke of luck—because I suggested that two weekends from then I come down to New York and we go to the circus. I didn't know then, but of course that was a passion with her. She went every year at least once. So we went to the circus.

GS: Well, what tone did she take when she found out you were seriously considering giving four years of your life to medicine?

EB: Actually, I didn't tell her I wrote for a long time. Maybe I hadn't even told her then. I guess she must have known by the time I graduated. Even then—I suppose this was a little odd even then—we called each other Miss for about three years. I admired her very much, and still do, of course.

She had a review of Wallace Stevens that I don't think she ever reprinted. I went over there (to Brooklyn) and I went in through the back door (the elevator wasn't working). There were two of those baskets for tomatoes, bushel baskets, filled with papers, inside the back door. These were the first drafts of the rather short review. You can see how hard she worked.

She had a clip-board that she carried around the house to work on a poem while she was washing dishes, dusting, etc. . . .

Now all her papers, or almost all, are in the Berg Museum in Philadelphia. They have everything there, in fact they've reconstructed her New York living room and bedroom. I went to the opening and found it all rather painful. But the exhibit of manuscripts was marvelous. If ever you want to see examples of real work, study her manuscripts.

She wrote a poem about the famous racehorse, Tom Fool. The man who arranged the collection had done a beautiful job, in glass cases: dozens of little clippings from the newspapers and photographs of the horse. And then the versions of the poem. It goes on and on . . . The work she put in!

GS: I'd be fascinated to see how she did those inaudible rhymes—whether that came first, or kept changing. How that figured.

EB: She was rather contradictory, you know, illogical sometimes. She would say, "Oh—rhyme is dowdy." Then other times when she was translating La Fontaine she would ask me for a rhyme. If I could give her a rhyme, she would seem to be pleased. She liked a ballad of mine because it rhymed so well. She admired the rhyme "many antennae." You could never tell what she was going to like or dislike.

GS: But what an extraordinary stroke of good fortune to be a friend of Miss Moore's before she knew that you had ambitions . . .

EB: Oh, I didn't have many ambitions. As I said, I must have been half-asleep. There was an anthology that came out, with ten or twelve young poets—in 1935, I think. Each of us "young" poets had an older poet write an introduction. With great timidity I asked Marianne, and she did write a few paragraphs. And she disapproved very much of some of my language and said so, too. It is very funny. I think only one of those poems was in my first book.

The first reading of hers I ever went to, in Brooklyn, years ago, she read with William Carlos Williams. I think at that time she had given very few readings. It was in a church, I think, in a basement. It was a sort of sloping, small auditorium, very steep, and Miss Moore and Dr. Williams were sitting on Victorian Gothic chairs, with red plush backs, on either side of a platform with what looked like a small pulpit at the front. I went over on the subway and was a little late. I had planned to be there early but I was late. Marianne was reading. I was making my way down the red carpeted steps to the front—there were very few people there—and she looked up, noticed me, nodded politely and said "Good evening!" Then went right on reading. She and Dr. Williams were very nice with each other. I don't remember very much else about it, what they read, oh, except a young woman who is editing Williams's letters sent me a copy a month or so ago of something she had run across: a letter from Williams about this very same evening. And it says "Marianne Moore had a little girl named Elizabeth Bishop in tow. It seems she writes poetry." Something like that. Of course I never knew Dr. Williams very well.

GS: But you knew Lowell, Jarrell, so many of them . . .

EB: You know I think we all think this about everybody—every other poet. I didn't know a soul. That is, no one "literary" except Miss Moore at that time.

GS: When did you meet Lowell? I ask this because the way he brought your works into a writing class I visited once at B. U. some years ago, I had the feeling that he had known you and your work . . .

EB: In 1945 or 1946 I met Randall Jarrell, I can't remember how or where. He came to New York that winter to take Margaret Marshall's place on *The Nation* as book review editor. She left the Jarrells her apartment. I had just published my first book, and Robert Lowell had just published his first book. Randall had known him at Kenyon College. Randall invited me to dinner to meet him and we got along immediately. I'd read *Lord Weary's Castle,* but that wasn't it. For some reason we just hit it off very well. By chance we'd been to see the same art exhibits that afternoon and we talked about those. Almost everybody has this theory that everybody else has a fascinating social life . . .

GS: Did you meet [Reed] Whittemore? He was so active, as an editor, with *Furioso* . . .

EB: I never met him.

GS: Did you meet Berryman?

EB: No, I never met him. I've met more writers in the last three or four years than I had in all the rest of my life put together.

GS: And Brazilian writers?

EB: I didn't meet any of them. I know a few. The one I admire most of the older generation is Carlos Drummond de Andrade, I've translated him. I didn't know him at all. He's supposed to be very shy. I'm supposed to be very shy. We've met once—on the sidewalk at night. We had just come out of the same restaurant, and he kissed my hand politely when we were introduced.

I do know a few of the others. Vinicius de Moraes, who wrote *Black Orpheus.* He was a very good poet, a serious one, somewhat Eliot-ish. He still is, but now he writes mostly popular songs, very good ones—"Girl from Ipanema," for example, an old one now. He plays the guitar and sings well, but without much voice, really. He's very popular with the young. He's been a very good friend to me. He gets married rather frequently. He says: "All my wives are such wonderful girls. It's always all my fault. Of course I'm broke. I leave them everything, and just take a toothbrush and go." One funny story: I was staying in the little town where I had bought an old, old house. It wasn't ready to move in to (that took five or six years) and I was staying at a small inn, owned by a Danish woman, an old friend. Vinicius was there, too—just the three of us. It was winter, cold and rainy, dreadful weather. We sat, for warmth, just the three of us, in a sort of back-kitchen, reserved for friends, all day long, and read detective stories. Once in a while we'd play a game of cards or

Vinicius would play his guitar and sing. He has some marvelous, charming songs for children. Well, every afternoon a Rio newspaper arrived, one with a gossip column we read avidly. So, one afternoon the boy came in with the newspaper and there was a big gossip piece in it about the very same little town we were in, how it had become "fashionable with the intellectuals." And there we were, the only "intellectuals," if that, within hundreds of miles, handing around our Agatha Christies and Rex Stouts and so on . . .

GS: You seem to write more and more kinds of poems but without exhorting yourself to be suddenly different.

EB: I know I wish I had written a great deal more. Sometimes I think if I had been born a man I probably would have written more. Dared more, or been able to spend more time at it. I've wasted a great deal of time.

GS: Would it have been extra works in other genres?

EB: No.

GS: Long poems?

EB: No. One or two long poems I'd like to write, but I doubt that I ever shall. Well, not really long. Maybe ten pages. That'd be long.

Yes, I did know Cummings some. When I lived in the Village, later on, I met him through a friend. He and I had the same maid for two or three years. "Leave a little dirt, Blanche," he used to say to her. Blanche finally left them. They wouldn't put traps down for the mice. Mrs. Cummings told her a story about a little mouse that would come out of the wall and get up on the bed. They would lie in bed and watch her roll up little balls of wool from the blanket, to make her nest. Well, Blanche was appalled at this.

GS: Was he sparing the mice on humanitarian or vegetarian principles?

EB: Oh no. Cummings loved mice. He wrote poems about mice. He adored them. He used to . . .

Well, I haven't said anything profound.

GS: You tell a wonderful story.

EB: Oh, in their interviews, Miss Moore always said something to make one think very hard about writing, about technique—and Lowell always says something I find mysterious . . .

GS: Would you like to say something mysterious?

EB: !

Geography of the Imagination

Alexandra Johnson / 1978

From the *Christian Science Monitor,* 23 March 1978, 20–21.
Reprinted by permission from the *Christian Science Monitor* ©
1978 The Christian Science Publishing Society. All rights reserved.

"More delicate than the historians are the map-makers' colors."
This line from "The Map," the first poem in Elizabeth Bishop's
first book, evokes the theme and the texture of her own work.
Miss Bishop's poems are delicately shaded maps which chart
with immaculate skill the geography of her imagination.

Recognized as one of today's most outstanding poets, her
work is hallmarked by its elegant simplicity and pristine crafts-
manship. Everything her eye—or mind's eye—turns to shows a
rare respect for the familiar world around her. In each poem,
we are made to notice something very basic, and therefore
mysterious, about the things which surround us. In short, her
poems offer a cool respite from much of the self-indulgent,
confessional poetry to which today's readers have become
increasingly accustomed.

Elizabeth Bishop's awards are legion. Among them are the
Pulitzer Prize, the National Book Award, the Academy of American Poets Award and the coveted Neustadt International Prize
for Literature.

Alexandra Johnson, the *Monitor's* Assistant Home Forum
Editor, interviewed Miss Bishop recently. The following com-
prises some of their discussion.

*Why do you write poetry? What about it, as a genre, appeals to you
over other writing forms?*

Well, who knows really? I began when I was very young, about
eight. I was very isolated as a child and perhaps poetry was my way
of making familiar what I saw around me. Many things probably
contributed to this. For example, my Nova Scotia grandmother was a
great hymn singer. I grew up with those sounds, and, in fact, still
have hundreds of them floating around my head. My aunt, like so
many Victorians, belonged to the village's poetry society and she
recited a great deal to me—Longfellow, Browning, Tennyson. So

obviously I memorized a lot and it soon became an unconscious part of me.

Poetry has always seemed the most natural way of saying what I feel. I never intended to "be" a poet, as I think people set out to do today. I never wanted to think about any label. It's far more important to just keep writing poetry than to think of yourself as a poet whose job is to write poetry all the time. What do such people do during those long, infertile periods? Poetry should be as unconscious as possible.

Does a poem begin for you with a sound, an Image or an Idea?

It differs with every single poem. Some poems begin as a set of words that you aren't sure what they apply to, but eventually they accumulate and become lines, and then you see some pattern emerge. Sometimes an idea haunts me for a long time, though poems that start as ideas are much harder to write. It's easier when they start out with a set of words that sound nice and don't make much sense but eventually reveal their purpose. Again, the unconscious quality is very important. You don't ask a poem what it means, you have to let it tell you.

How long do you carry a poem in your head before committing it to paper?

From 10 minutes to 40 years. One of the few good qualities I think I have as a poet is patience. I have endless patience. Sometimes I feel I should be angry at myself for being willing to wait 20 years for a poem to get finished, but I don't think a good poet can afford to be in a rush.

One thing I love about your poetry is its ability to render the ordinary extraordinary, to make us look again and again at the familiar. Is this a conscious motive on your part?

I'm not trying to do anything specific in my poetry—only to please myself. The greatest challenge, for me, is to try and express difficult thoughts in plain language. I prize clarity and simplicity. I like to present complicated or mysterious ideas in the simplest way possible. This is a discipline which many poets don't see as important as I do. Complexity, I think, often obscures fuzzy thinking or verse masking as poetry. If poetry isn't disciplined then probably the eye which observed or the mind which translated the experience lacked a certain discipline.

One senses that you are not observing an object for the first time, but rather returning to it again and again to capture its "otherness." Will you comment?

I am very object-struck. Critics have often written that I write more about things than people. This isn't conscious on my part. I simply try to see things afresh. A certain curiosity about the world around you is one of the most important things in life. It's behind almost all poetry.

I am very fond of painting and this may account for some of my interest in observing things closely. My aunts sketched and painted watercolors and this may have subtly influenced me. In fact, I often wish I had been born a painter rather than a writer.

What sources feed you?

Inspiration is a very curious word. When I was living in Brazil, I had a study up on the side of a mountain that overlooked a waterfall and a small pool beneath it. Around it was a clump of royal bamboo. When visitors came, many of whom had never read a single line I had written, they would point to the bamboo and say, "So this is where you get your inspiration!" I thought at one point of pinning a sign on the bamboo saying, "Inspiration."

This mysterious thing we call Inspiration isn't that easy to pinpoint. But it's the strange and wonderful thing about writing poetry—you can never predict where or when or even why something moves you to write a poem. That's what I mean when I said a poem comes in many guises. A poem may be inspired by something that happened 20 years ago but until I've written it, I may not have realized that at the time I was greatly moved. I think you have a trust that the eye and mind are constantly recording, and be patient enough for them to reveal what they have observed.

Your poems show a respect for seemingly ordinary things—a fish, a moose, a filling station even. Can one say: to respect is to see and to see is to respect?

I have a great interest and respect, if you like, for what people call ordinary things. I am very visually minded and mooses and filling stations aren't necessarily commonplace to me. Observation is a great joy. Some critics charge that I'm merely a descriptive poet which I don't think is such a bad thing at all if you've done it well.

I've always been fascinated by your line, "Is it lack of imagination that makes us come to imagined places—not just stay at home?" Would you elaborate on this line?
I was really poking fun at myself with that line, or at anyone who doesn't trust his initial view of something. Any place has to be different from the way you imagined it, but that doesn't mean what you imagined is in any way inferior. The imagination does have its own geography.

Would you rather journey in person or through writing a poem?
Oh, in travel. It's so much easier! But as a poet, I guess I do both. They are very different, though.

Did living in Brazil help to discipline and mature your poetry by forcing you back on your own sense of language?
No, I don't think living in a foreign country does that. You're going to have to discover the discipline wherever you are. It can be done as easily in your own country at your own desk, however unromantic that seems. This is part of the mystique of inspiration—that you believe it's found outside yourself. The more exotic the context, some people feel, the more unusual the work. But I don't think they have much to do with each other.

Your poems employ extensive imagery of maps and geography. Could you discuss why?
Well, my mother's family wandered a lot and loved this strange world of travel. My first poem in my first book was inspired when I was sitting on the floor, one New Year's Eve in Greenwich Village, after I graduated from college. I was staring at a map. The poem wrote itself. People will say that it corresponded to some part of me which I was unaware of at the time. This may be true.

Geography III, *in part, concerns itself with the search for and definition of home. Is writing poetry your way of finding or having that home?*
Interestingly enough, many of those poems were written when I

decided to leave Brazil where I had lived for a long time. This may have contributed to this feeling. I've never felt particularly homeless, but, then, I've never felt particularly at home. I guess that's a pretty good description of a poet's sense of home. He carries it within him.

In "Crusoe in England" you write about a man who was forced to record every flora and fauna. Is this intended to suggest the poet's duty or his burden?

I'm not sure. It's true that many poets don't like the fact that they have to translate everything into words. There is a certain self-mockery, I guess.

Are you surprised by how people interpret or overinterpret your work?

Astounded! But more so earlier than now; criticism has become a commonplace thing. Occasionally, I'll read what a person has to say about my work—such as this thing in the *New Yorker* which just came. I think it's totally wrong. Other times, I'll reflect and say, "That could be." People continually point out interesting things and are very disappointed to hear that I hadn't been thinking that way at all.

Octavio Paz, who is a poet and friend I admire a great deal, gave a poetry class which I attended. The first day he told the class he didn't want them to read any criticism, which I also agree with wholeheartedly. When asked why, he responded rather wryly, "Critics have so much more active imaginations than poets." I found this very amusing and accurate.

You have resisted almost every temptation to which both good and bad poets yield today—such as confessional or obscurely structural poetry. Have you always had a true sense of your poetic voice?

No, I haven't. This used to worry me a great deal and still does. In my first book, I was worried that none of the poems went together, that there was no discernible theme. I feel this about everything I've ever done. But apparently there is a consistent voice. I am grateful but astounded to hear this.

Yet in almost every poem one hears the calm, consistent voice of Elizabeth Bishop. Does this happen naturally, then?

Well, I'm not calm, but it's nice to hear! I never think of any tone when writing. It just comes, I guess.

On the Monitor, *we receive hundreds of poems a week from people of all ages and backgrounds. Would you comment on why poetry is suddenly flourishing today?*

It's incredible, isn't it? Magazines, readings, courses! When I began teaching, I was asked to select 10 students which was very hard. But every year there were more and more applicants though other literature courses were dwindling.

Many students have the mistaken idea that poetry is an easy course. Though they probably know, in my case, that I don't believe you can give marks for poetry. But going deeper, I think people are feeling so desperate in other areas of their life—how to reconcile making a living when you want to write poetry, for example—that they turn to these classes when they can. Poetry, for better or worse, has become an outlet for conflicts

I get an average of ten poetry books or manuscripts a week. Many of them sound alike. Auden would have said this is because of free verse. And he might have been right. But a great deal is slap-dash. I don't necessarily like strict form, but too much poetry today lacks coherency.

People may be writing because they don't know where else to turn to. Institutions, they think, have failed them, so they turn inward. T. S. Eliot, though, was right, I think, when he said that the more you try to express yourself, the less you really express. So much poetry I see seems self-indulgent. I feel people don't get enough out of the *original* experience that prompted a poem. The essential experience, the living of life if you like, appears to be missing or incomplete. Are people writing more because they're living less fully? Who knows. This isn't the aim or purpose of poetry, though. Poetry should celebrate what you see, not necessarily lament what you haven't seen.

How do you counsel young poets who find it difficult to "justify" writing poetry as a full-time occupation?

I ask to see some of their work. But, then, you can't always tell from the work. Someone who writes poorly in college may surprise you in a couple of years. This is why I don't like to give grades in college classes. A low mark may discourage the person who has yet to find his or her voice and may succeed in doing so in a few years. But, frankly, I feel that the true poetic genius wouldn't come near a poetry class. He's probably off writing—though that may not be entirely true. I've had the good fortune to encounter at least four really talented people in classes.

A luxuriant romanticism has grown up around how a poet should live and work. How necessary is that quiet, circumscribed life?

Well, you get a place all set up, as I've done only one time in my life, which was in Brazil. You have your books and pencils and papers ready. Then you find yourself writing some of your best lines standing up in the kitchen putting them on the back of an old envelope. This happened to me over and over. Inspiration isn't restricted to just one quiet room.

A final question: What one quality should every poem have?

Surprise. The subject and the language which conveys it should surprise you. You should be surprised at seeing something new and strangely alive.

Elizabeth Bishop, Observer
of Poetry

Joan Zyda / 1978

Reprinted from the *Chicago Tribune,* 4 June 1978, section 5, 4.

Elizabeth Bishop, the grande dame of American poetry, has read
much of the new women's poetry. "Some of it is good, and some of
it is terrible."

In particular, she says some of the new love poems and erotic
poems by women are "courageous and fun," but some of the angrier
feminist poems are "cruel and ugly."

But on the whole, she says, "Poetry shouldn't be used as a vehicle
for any personal philosophy."

She often is called an "eye" or "map-maker" poet. Her poems
give meticulously detailed descriptions of geography—seascapes,
flora, fauna, and houses. In her latest book, *Geography III* (Farrar,
$7.95), she writes of a map where "peninsulas take water between
thumb and finger/like women feeling for the smoothness of yard
goods"; and a storm "roaming the sky uneasily/like a dog looking for
a place to sleep in."

Such poetry has won Bishop an impressive assortment of prizes,
including the Pulitzer in 1955, the National Book Award in 1969, and
the National Book Critics Circle poetry award last year. In 1976, she
became the first American and first woman to win the prestigious
Books Abroad/Neustadt International Prize for Literature. And that
same year, she was elected to the elite American Academy of Arts
and Letters.

Now 67, Bishop has been observing and writing poems for more
than half a century—"since I was 8," she said, adding "Oh, I
stopped—I had writer's blocks when I was 12 and 17."

Born the daughter of a well-to-do Massachusetts builder, Bishop
began publishing while at Vassar College.

After college, Bishop set out on the travels that would provide
many of the particulars of her imagery. She lingered (on a private

income and poetry prize money) in New York, Newfoundland, France, Spain, North Africa, Ireland, and Italy. She also lived in Nova Scotia, New England, Florida, Mexico, and Brazil. Her longest stay was in Petrópolis, Brazil, from 1952 to 1968.

Away from the United States and the fashionable ideological and technical novelties of much post-World War II poetry, Bishop pursued her distinctive style.

"Her work is not easily labeled," wrote Howard Moss, poetry editor of *New Yorker* magazine. "She is not academic, beat, cooked, raw, formal, informal, metrical, or syllabic. . . . She is a poet, pure and simple, who has perfect pitch."

Bishop now lives in Boston, close to the coastline she has made familiar to her readers, in a renovated granite warehouse built in 1848. For the last seven years, she has been the poet-in-residence at Harvard University.

She says criticism of her own work doesn't bother her. But she is very sensitive about accusations that she is antifeminist for refusing to let her work appear in anthologies of women poets.

"I've always considered myself a strong feminist," Bishop says. "It's absurd to segregate the sexes that way. It's also silly to have shows for women photographers, women opera singers, and so forth. Would you bother to go to a show that's billed, 'Best Male Photographers'? It's just plain silly."

Nevertheless, Bishop has suffered mild patronization of her work from reviewers. "Some of the most wonderful reviews I've had have been ruined because at the end they'll say, 'This is the best book by a woman in this decade.' I've been taking that all my life," she says. "All I can do is take it with a touch of irony."

Elizabeth Bishop Speaks about Her Poetry

Eileen McMahon / 1978

Reprinted from *The New Paper* (Bennington College), 4 (June 1978), 1, 6.

Elizabeth Bishop and I met for breakfast and for an interview the morning after her reading at the college. In the course of discussing whether or not the blueberry pancakes might be any good, we discovered a common interest in the Maine islands. From there on our conversation centered around tales of our summer adventures, sailing and living on the Cape and in Maine.

I have transcribed those parts that I hope reveal most about the poet and her poetic voice.

Q. I understand that you interviewed T.S. Eliot when you were a student at Vassar. How did that interview come about?

A. It was very funny. I was on the newspaper and I think I was a sophomore. I don't know why I was on the newspaper, but I was all the time. I used to go to the meetings, although I didn't really do all that much news—it took a lot of time.

The office had a big long table that we would all sit around while different people wrote different things. I used to desert the meetings almost immediately and go across the street to a place called "The Popover Shop." There I would sit and write these awful brief humorous bits, or editorials, or poems—funny poems.

I think the editor-in-chief, Eleanor Clark's sister, very nobly thought that because I had published a couple of poems I should be the one to interview Eliot.

I was absolutely scared to death—just sick. I got rather dressed up. I can just see it: I had on a summer suit that I wore with spectator sport shoes. It was a blazing hot day, just terrible. At the time the honorable guests were put up in Andrew Vassar's suite. It was full of wonderful old Victorian stuff. Eliot and I sat on a horse hair sofa. I remember my legs were too short and I kept sliding off the sofa. He looked exhausted and sat mopping his brow. He had given a talk that afternoon. It was very good, I can remember some of it still. I think he finally asked me if I would mind if he undid his tie, which for Eliot was rather like taking off all his clothes.

I can't say I ever felt at ease, but he was extremely nice. A group of us had started a little magazine on our own because the college magazine would not print anything we wrote. Somehow Eliot heard about this, I don't know how, and he asked me about it. He requested three copies, and wrote a nice note about them. Later the official magazine gave in and decided they would have to print us.

Q. *In an interview with George Starbuck you were quoted as saying: "Sometimes I think if I had been born a man I probably would have written more. Dared more."*

A. Oh, yes. Well, I think George was trying terribly hard to get me to say something pro-feminist or anti-feminist. Possibly because I was well received when I was young, for I feel that I have not written as much as I might have if I had been a man.

Q. *Do you feel that there is something in a woman's perception of life as an observer that makes her poetry different from a man's?*

A. Women's experiences are much more limited, but that does not really matter—there is Emily Dickinson, as one always says. You just have to make do with what you have after all.

It depends on one's temperament I suppose. Some women certainly can write like Emily Dickinson, the kind of poetry with no common experience to speak of at all, where there may be some women dying to get out and climb Mt. Everest. They do I guess. They feel that they have not lived until they have done all these things, which is, of course, a lot of nonsense.

Q. *Do you think that there is one particular poem that carries the full range of your voice?*

A. I don't know. Who am I to say? Most poems, if you like them, finally add up to say more than you realize. I think that everyone, when he publishes his first book, or even later, thinks that these poems are all very well, but there is no reason for them to go together. Eventually they see that there is an underlying thread. Of course, critics find the most extraordinary philosophies that never could have occurred to you when you wrote the poem.

Q. *Do you think that the Latin and Greek you studied in college affected your poetry?*

A. Latin probably. I had an excellent teacher while I was at Vassar. I remember sitting for a couple of years on Monday mornings and writing Latin prose from English prose. I was not a very good student in college. I was always distracted, but I do think that Latin is probably the best writing exercise I can think of.

Evelyn Waugh has a very good passage in his first autobiography about the value of translation both ways—from a dead language to live ones. Through translation you learn that certain words mean things and they have to be in certain places in a sentence to be effective.

Q. *Ben Belitt teaches one of the Verse Workshops here at Bennington College. How well do you know him?*

A. Oh yes, I have known Ben for a number of years. I knew him from Key West. My memories go back further than his do. The first year he was there I remember him walking down the sidewalk in the early morning and telling me: "I have written 40 lines this morning." Now he says that he never said such a thing. Well, he did. He said that he wrote 40 lines every day. I was just dumb-founded.

Q. *How often do you write?*

A. Some days all I do is write and then for months I don't write a thing.

Q. *How did it happen that you dedicated the poem "The Armadillo" to Robert Lowell?*

A. I visited Lowell in Castine, Maine in 1957 when I was up from Brazil with a Brazilian friend of mine. The skunk business was going on then at the back door, where we saw it with a flashlight. Then he wrote "Skunk Hour." I had already written "The Armadillo" and he thought his poem was influenced by mine, which it isn't at all. It is a totally different thing, very serious. I was about to have a book out and he was about to have a book out. I thought I would like to have something to dedicate to him, since the skunk poem was so beautiful, but I really did not have anything. So I dedicated "The Armadillo" to him after I wrote it. I think it is awfully funny. Marianne Moore has a poem to her dearest friend, Hildergarde Watson, called "The Wood Weasel." If you read the initial letters up from the bottom it reads: Hildergarde Watson. So I think this is really odd when people dedicate poems to the ones that they love when they are about skunks—I know two cases now.

Q. *When did you first meet Randall Jarrell?*

A. Well, he was in New York for the winter of '47. He rented an apartment from Margaret Marshall, who at the time was the Literary Editor of *The Nation,* when she took a year off. I think I met him at a reading. Anyway we met and became quite friendly.

Q. *I came across your poem, "Wading at Wellfleet." I am curious to know how much time you spent on the Cape?*

A. I liked the Cape so much when I was in my teens there. The Cape is so different now though. I went to a sailing camp in Wellfleet from the time I was 12 until I was 18. It does not exist now, but it was wonderful then. What I did like best about it was the sailing. I went back there a couple of summers when I was in college and rented a little house near the railroad track for $25 a month. I rented a boat those two summers, but I have not done much sailing since.

I went down in '51 to visit Randall Jarrell, who rented a house for the summer in Orleans. He drove me down to Provincetown one day and by then the whole Cape had changed so much I swore I would never go back. I never have gone back.

Women Writers in America
Sheila Hale / 1978

Excerpted from *Harpers and Queen* (July 1978), 61–62.

Boston might seem the appropriate place to meet Elizabeth Bishop. She was born nearby in Worcester, Massachusetts. She has the retiring manner and self-protective humour of a native New Englander. But unlike her friend Robert Lowell—who acknowledged her influence and whom she now succeeds, in the view of most serious critics, as the most important living American poet—she is attached to New England neither by deep roots nor by temperament. She spent the early years of her childhood in Nova Scotia. And she speaks with special affection of two of her Canadian ancestors: the painter George Hutchinson RA, and William Hutchinson, "a sea captain who sailed around the Horn to Rio along exactly the same route I took when I first went there though I didn't know at the time." Since 1952 she has chosen to live mostly in Brazil.

She is in Boston now, "because prices went up in Brazil" and she was induced to accept a job at Harvard teaching Advanced Verse Writing. But she is relieved that at 67 she has now reached retirement age. "The whole thing was a lot of nonsense. There is so little you can teach them. The ones who have talent would be better off sitting in a corner reading poetry; those who don't might as well study economics. I begged to be allowed to teach prose because in America even graduate students can't string five grammatical sentences together much less write verse. One of my students was a football hero, who wrote quite well to my surprise. But the only ones who had studied English grammar were foreigners. American poetry is very lively just now. We have better poets than England (although English journalism is *much* better), but I don't think that has anything to do with all these creative writing courses. How I hate that word Creative!"

She has filled her apartment, in a beautifully converted warehouse on the Waterfront, with possessions which remind her of more interesting times and places: the wooden figurehead from an old Brazilian

sailing ship, the plaster feather quill from an Italian statue of Santa
Barbara (patron saint of writers), the travel books which are her
preferred reading. It will come as no surprise to anyone who knows
Elizabeth Bishop's poetry to learn that she is an accomplished painter
and musician. Given another life, she says, she would have chosen
painting over poetry. "It's a healthier life, and painters are much
nicer than literary people. When I went to Vassar I wanted to
compose. Then I decided to become a doctor after college. I would
have liked to do something practical and useful with my life; I
certainly never *intended* to become a poet. But with me things just
sort of happen."

The poetry began to happen when she was "seven or eight or
nine." As a child she suffered from the chronic asthma which has
plagued her all her life. "I lay around wheezing and reading for years.
Then I discovered the metaphysical poets: George Herbert, especially, has been the most important and lasting influence on me.
Coleridge said about him (in a book I found in a secondhand bookshop
when I was fourteen or fifteen) that he wrote about the most fantastic
things imaginable in perfectly simple everyday language. That is what
I've always tried to do. Although I did go through a period of writing
bad Hopkins—elaborate rhymes and meters—after a friend at summer
camp gave me an anthology with twelve lines of Hopkins who was
then otherwise not in print here.

"Auden influenced everybody when I was at college. Or he didn't.
What you couldn't do was ignore him. Then I met Marianne Moore.
Mrs. Fanny Borden, the librarian at Vassar, introduced us in the New
York Public Library. Mary Moore always met people outside the
reading-room door so she could escape from them. She was forty and
I was twenty-one and I was petrified; but we just seemed to hit it off.
She had an amazing personality and my first books were influenced
by her, especially the subject matter. But that connection has been
overdone by reviewers. She was a syllabic poet. I'm more oompad-
iooom.

"Mary McCarthy was one year ahead of me at Vassar (I'm very
particular about that year's difference). Fanny Borden is Helena's
mother in *The Group*. I couldn't say for certain that I'm *not* in *The
Group*—most of those women were a mixture of real people. But I
wasn't as affected by the Depression as some of my contemporaries;
not as much as my friends said I should have been. I've always been

more interested in visual things than politics. But I was, and am, a feminist; and that is why I refuse absolutely to contribute to all-women volumes or all-women readings.

"I absolutely *hate* reading my work aloud under any circumstances. The first time I gave a reading I stopped for twenty-six years. Harvard is a terrible place for reading; they are famous for being cold and you feel your voice getting deader and deader. The further west you go, the better the audiences, because they're not showing off. The nicest audience I ever had was children (at the American school in Rio). They asked such good questions, like, Why did you choose this word instead of that. Simple, practical things, which is the way you write, of course."

The Art of Poetry, XXVII: Elizabeth Bishop

Elizabeth Spires / 1978

Reprinted from the *Paris Review*, 23 (Summer 1981), 56–83.
From *Writers at Work*, Sixth Series by George A. Plimpton,
Editor. Copyright © 1984 The Paris Review, Inc. Used by
permission of Viking Penguin, a division of Penguin Books
USA, Inc.

The interview took place at Lewis Wharf, Boston, on the
afternoon of June 28, 1978, three days before Miss Bishop and
two friends were to leave for North Haven, a Maine island in
Penobscot Bay where she summered. Her living room, on the
fourth floor of Lewis Wharf, had a spectacular view of Boston
Harbor; when I arrived, she immediately took me out on the
balcony to point out such Boston landmarks as Old North
Church in the distance, mentioning that "Old Ironsides" was
moored nearby.

Her living room was spacious and attractive, with wide-
planked polished floors, a beamed ceiling, two old brick walls,
and one wall of books. Besides some comfortable modern
furniture, the room included a jacaranda rocker and other old
pieces from Brazil, two paintings by Loren MacIver, a giant
horse conch from Key West, and a Franklin stove with firewood
in a donkey pannier, also from Brazil. The most conspicuous
piece was a large carved figurehead of an unknown beast, open-
mouthed, with horns and blue eyes, which hung on one wall
below the ceiling.

Her study, a smaller room down the hall, was in a state of
disorder. Literary magazines, books, and papers were piled
everywhere. Photographs of Marianne Moore, Robert Lowell,
and other friends hung on the walls; one of Dom Pedro, the last
emperor of Brazil, she especially liked to show to her Brazilian
visitors. "Most have no idea who he is," she said. "This is after
he abdicated and shortly before he died—he looked very sad."
Her desk was tucked in a far corner by the only window, also
with a north view of the harbor.

At sixty-seven, Miss Bishop was easily and accurately described by the word "striking," her short, swept-back white
hair setting off an unforgettably noble face. She was wearing a
black tunic shirt, gold watch and earrings, gray slacks, and flat
brown Japanese sandals which made her appear shorter than
her actual height: five feet, four inches. Although she looked

well and was in high spirits, she complained of having had a recent hay fever attack and declined to have her photograph taken with the wry comment, "Photographers, insurance salesmen, and funeral directors are the worst forms of life."

Seven or eight months later, after reading a profile I had written for *The Vassar Quarterly* (which had been based on this interview) and worrying that she sounded like "the soul of frivolity," she wrote me: "I once admired an interview with Fred Astaire in which he refused to discuss 'the dance,' his partners, or his 'career' and stuck determinedly to golf—so I hope that some readers will realize I do think about ART once in a while even if babbling along like a very shallow brook . . . "

Note: Though Miss Bishop did have the opportunity of correcting those portions of this interview incorporated in the *Vassar Quarterly* article, she never saw it in this form.

Interviewer: Your living room seems to be a wonderful combination of the old and new. Is there a story behind any of the pieces, especially that figurehead? It's quite imposing.

Bishop: I lived in an extremely modern house in Brazil. It was very beautiful and when I finally moved I brought back things I liked best. So it's just a kind of mixture. I really like modern things but while I was there I acquired so many other things I couldn't bear to give them up. This figurehead is from the São Francisco River. Some are more beautiful; this is a very ugly one.

Interviewer: Is it supposed to ward off evil spirits?

Bishop: Yes, I think so. They were used for about fifty years on one section, two or three hundred miles, of the river. It's nothing compared to the Amazon but it's the next biggest river in Brazil. This figurehead is primitive folk art. I think I even know who made it. There was a black man who carved twenty or thirty, and it's exactly his style. Some of them are made of much more beautiful wood. There's a famous one called "The Red Horse" made of jacaranda. It's beautiful, a great thing like this one, a horse with its mouth open, but for some reason they all just disappeared. I made a week-long trip on that river in 1967 and didn't see one. The riverboat, a sternwheeler, had been built in 1880—something for the Mississippi, and you can't believe how tiny it was. We splashed along slowly for days and days . . . a very funny trip.

Interviewer: Did you spend so much of your life traveling because you were looking for a perfect place?

Bishop: No, I don't think so. I really haven't traveled that much. It just happened that although I wasn't rich I had a very small income from my father, who died when I was eight months old, and it was enough when I got out of college to go places on. And I traveled extremely cheaply. I could get along in Brazil for some years but now I couldn't possibly live on it. But the biographical sketch in the first anthology I was in said, "Oh, she's been to Morocco, Spain, etc.," and this has been repeated for years even though I haven't been back to any of these places. But I never traveled the way students travel now. Compared to my students, who seem to go to Nepal every Easter vacation, I haven't been anywhere at all.

Interviewer: Well, it always sounds as if you're very adventurous.

Bishop: I want to do the Upper Amazon. Maybe I will. You start from Peru and go down—

Interviewer: Do you write when you're actually traveling?

Bishop: Yes, sometimes. It depends. I usually take notes but not always. And I keep a kind of diary. The two trips I've made that I liked best were the Amazon trip and one to the Galapagos Islands three or four years ago . . . I'd like very much to go back to Italy again because I haven't seen nearly enough of it. And Sicily. Venice is wonderful. Florence is rather strenuous, I think. I was last there in '64 with my Brazilian friend. We rented a car and did northern Italy for five or six weeks. We didn't go to Rome. I *must* go back. There are so many things I haven't seen yet. I like painting probably better than I like poetry. And I haven't been back to Paris for years. I don't like the prices!

Interviewer: You mentioned earlier that you're leaving for North Haven in several days. Will this be a "working vacation"?

Bishop: This summer I want to do a lot of work because I really haven't done anything for ages and there are a couple of things I'd like to finish before I die. Two or three poems and two long stories. Maybe three. I sometimes feel that I shouldn't keep going back to this place that I found just by chance through an ad in the Harvard *Crimson*. I should probably go to see some more art, cathedrals, and so on. But I'm so crazy about it that I keep going back. You can see the water, a great expanse of water and fields from the house. Islands are beautiful. Some of them come right up, granite, and then dark firs. North Haven isn't like that exactly, but it's very beautiful. The island is sparsely inhabited and a lot of the people who have homes there are fearfully rich. Probably if it weren't for these people the island would be deserted the way a great many Maine islands are, because the village is very tiny. But the inhabitants almost all work—they're lobstermen but they work as caretakers. . . . The electricity there is rather sketchy. Two summers ago it was one hour on, one hour off. There I was with *two* electric typewriters and I couldn't keep working. There was a cartoon in the grocery store—it's eighteen miles from the mainland—a man in a hardware store saying, "I want an extension cord eighteen miles long!" Last year they did plug into the mainland—they put in cables. But once in a while the power still goes off.

Interviewer: So you compose on the typewriter?

Bishop: I can write prose on a typewriter. Not poetry. Nobody can read my writing so I write letters on it. And I've finally trained myself so I can write prose on it and then correct a great deal. But for poetry I use a pen. About halfway through sometimes I'll type out a few lines to see how they look.

William Carlos Williams wrote entirely on the typewriter. Robert Lowell printed—he never learned to write. He printed everything.

Interviewer: You've never been as prolific as many of your contemporaries. Do you start a lot of poems and finish very few?

Bishop: Yes. Alas, yes. I begin lots of things and then I give up on them. The last few years I haven't written as much because of teaching. I'm hoping that now that I'm free and have a Guggenheim I'll do a lot more.

Interviewer: How long did it take you to finish "The Moose"?

Bishop: That was funny. I started that *years* ago—twenty years ago, at least—I had a stack of notes, the first two or three stanzas, and the last.

Interviewer: It's such a dreamy poem. It seems to move the way a bus moves.

Bishop: It was all true. The bus trip took place before I went to Brazil. I went up to visit my aunt. Actually, I was on the wrong bus. I went to the right place but it wasn't the express I was supposed to get. It went roundabout and it was all exactly the way I described it, except that I say "seven relatives." Well, they weren't really relatives, they were various stepsons and so on, but that's the only thing that isn't quite true. I wanted to finish it because I liked it, but I could never seem to get the middle part, to get from one place to the other. And then when I was still living in Cambridge I was asked to give the Phi Beta Kappa poem at Harvard. I was rather pleased and I remembered that I had another unfinished poem. It's about whales and it was written a long time ago, too. I'm afraid I'll never publish it because it looks as if I were just trying to be up-to-date now that whales are a "cause."

Interviewer: But it's finished now?

Bishop: I think I could finish it very easily. I'm going to take it to Maine with me. I think I'll date it or nobody will believe I started it so long ago. At the time, though, I couldn't find the one about whales—this was in '73 or '74, I think—so I dug out "The Moose" and thought, "Maybe I can finish it," and I did. The day of the ceremony for Phi Beta Kappa (which I'd never made in college) we were all sitting on the platform at Sanders Theater. And the man who had asked me to give the poem leaned across the president and said to me whispering, "What is the name of your poem?" I said, " 'The Moose,' M-o-o-s-e," and he got up and introduced me and said, "Miss Bishop will now read a poem called, 'The *Moos*.' " Well, I choked and my hat was too big. And later the newspaper account read, "Miss Bishop read a poem called 'The Moose' and the tassle of her mortarboard swung back and forth over her face like a windshield wiper"!

The Glee Club was behind us and they sang rather badly, I thought, everybody thought. A friend of mine who couldn't come to this occasion but worked in one of the Harvard houses and knew some of the boys in the Glee Club asked one of them when they came back in their red jackets, "Well, how was it?" He said, "Oh, it was all right but we didn't sing well"—which was true—and then he said, "A woman read a poem." My friend said, "How was it?" And he said, "Well, as poems go, it wasn't bad"!

Interviewer: Have you ever had any poems that were gifts? Poems that seemed to write themselves?

Bishop: Oh yes. Once in awhile it happens. I wanted to write a villanelle all my life but I never could. I'd start them but for some reason I never could finish them. And one day I couldn't believe it—it was like writing a letter.* There was one rhyme I couldn't get that

---

*The poem is "One Art," in *Geography III*.

ended in e-n-t and a friend of mine, the poet Frank Bidart, came to
see me and I said, "Frank, give me a rhyme." He gave me a word
offhand and I put it in. But neither he nor I can remember which word
it was. But that kind of thing doesn't happen very often. Maybe some
poets always write that way. I don't know.

Interviewer: Didn't you used to give Marianne Moore rhymes?

Bishop: Yes, when she was doing the La Fontaine translations.
She'd call me up and read me something when I was in New York—I
was in Brazil most of that time—and say she needed a rhyme. She
said that she admired rhymes and meters very much. It was hard to
tell whether she was pulling your leg or not sometimes. She was Celtic
enough to be somewhat mysterious about these things.

Interviewer: Critics often talk about your more recent poems being
less formal, more "open," so to speak. They point out that *Geography III* has more of "you" in it, a wider emotional range. Do you
agree with these perceptions?

Bishop: This is what critics say. I've never written the things I'd
like to write that I've admired all my life. Maybe one never does.
Critics say the most incredible things!

Interviewer: I've been reading a critical book about you that Anne
Stevenson wrote. She said that in your poems nature was neutral.

Bishop: Yes, I remember the word "neutral." I wasn't quite sure
what she meant by that.

Interviewer: I thought she might have meant that if nature is neutral
there isn't any guiding spirit or force.

Bishop: Somebody famous—I can't think who it was—somebody
extremely famous was asked if he had one question to ask the Sphinx
and get an answer, what would it be? And he said, "Is nature for us
or against us?" Well, I've never really thought about it one way or the
other. I like the country, the seashore especially, and if I could drive,
I'd probably be living in the country. Unfortunately, I've never
learned to drive. I bought two cars. At least. I had an MG I adored
for some years in Brazil. We lived on top of a mountain peak, and it
took an hour to get somewhere where I could practice. And nobody
really had time to take an afternoon off and give me driving lessons.
So I never got my license. And I *never* would have driven in Rio,
anyway. But if you can't drive, you can't live in the country.

Interviewer: Do you have the painting here that your uncle did? The one "about the size of an old-style dollar bill" that you wrote about in "Poem"?

Bishop: Oh, sure. Do you want to see it? It's not good enough to hang. Actually, he was my great-uncle. I never met him.

Interviewer: The cows in this really are just one or two brush-strokes!

Bishop: I exaggerated a little bit. There's detail in the poem that isn't in the painting. I can't remember what it is now. My uncle did another painting when he was fourteen or fifteen years old that I wrote about in an early poem ["Large Bad Picture"]. An aunt who lived in Montreal had both of these and they used to hang in her front hall. I was dying to get them and I went there once and tried to buy them, but she wouldn't sell them to me. She was rather stingy. She died some years ago. I don't know who has the large one now.

Interviewer: When you were showing me your study, I noticed a shadow-box hanging in the hall. Is it by Joseph Cornell?

Bishop: No, I did that one. That's one of my little works. It's about infant mortality in Brazil. It's called *anjinhos,* which means "little angels." That's what they call the babies and small children who die.

Interviewer: What's the significance of the various objects?

Bishop: I found the child's sandal on a beach wading east of Rio one Christmas and I finally decided to do something with it. The pacifier was bright red rubber. They sell them in big bottles and jars in drugstores in Brazil. I decided it couldn't be red, so I dyed it black with India ink. A nephew of my Brazilian friend, a very smart young man, came to call while I was doing this. He brought two American rock-and-roll musicians and we talked and talked and talked, and I never thought to explain in all the time they were there what I was doing. When they left, I thought, "My God, they must think I'm a witch or something!"

Interviewer: What about the little bowls and skillets filled with rice?

Bishop: Oh, they're just things children would be playing with. And of course rice and black beans are what Brazilians eat every day.

Cornell is superb. I first saw the *Medici Slot Machine* when I was in college. Oh, I loved it. To think one could have *bought* some of those things then. He was very strange. He got crushes on opera singers and ballet dancers. When I looked at his show in New York two years ago I nearly fainted, because one of my favorite books is a

book he liked and used. It's a little book by an English scientist who
wrote for children about soap bubbles [*Soap Bubbles; their colours
and the forces which mold them,* by Sir C. V. Boys, 1889].

His sister began writing me after she read Octavio Paz's poem for
Cornell that I translated. (She doesn't read Spanish.) She sent me a
German-French grammar that apparently he meant to do something
with and never did. A lot of the pages were folded over and they're
all made into star patterns with red ink around them. . . . He lived in
what was called Elysian Park. That's an awfully strange address
to have.

Interviewer: Until recently, you were one of the few American
poets who didn't make their living teaching or giving readings. What
made you decide to start doing both?

Bishop: I never wanted to teach in my life. I finally did because I
wanted to leave Brazil and I needed the money. Since 1970 I've just
been *swamped* with people sending me poems. They start to when
they know you're in the country. I used to get them in Brazil, but not
so much. They got lost in the mail quite often. I don't believe in
teaching poetry at all, but that's what they want one to do. You see
so many poems every week, you just lose all sense of judgment.

As for readings, I gave a reading in 1947 at Wellesley College two
months after my first book appeared. And I was *sick* for days ahead
of time. Oh, it was absurd. And then I did one in Washington in '49
and I was sick again and nobody could hear me. And then I didn't
give any for twenty-six years. I don't mind reading now. I've gotten
over my shyness a little bit. I think teaching helps. I've noticed that
teachers aren't shy. They're rather aggressive. They get to be, finally.

Interviewer: Did you ever take a writing course as a student?

Bishop: When I went to Vassar I took sixteenth-century, seventeenth-century, and eighteenth-century literature, and then a course
in the novel. The kind of courses where you have to do a lot of
reading. I don't think I believe in writing courses at all. There weren't
any when I was there. There was a poetry-writing course in the
evening, but not for credit. A couple of my friends went to it, but I
never did.

The word "creative" drives me crazy. I don't like to regard it as
therapy. I was in the hospital several years ago and somebody gave
me Kenneth Koch's book, *Rose, Where Did You Get That Red?* And

it's true, children sometimes write wonderful things, paint wonderful pictures, but I think they should be *dis*couraged. From everything I've read and heard, the number of students in English departments taking literature courses has been falling off enormously. But at the same time the number of people who want to get in the writing classes seems to get bigger and bigger. There are usually two or three being given at Harvard every year. I'd get forty applicants for ten or twelve places. Fifty. It got bigger and bigger. I don't know if they do this to offset practical concerns, or what.

Interviewer: I think people want to be able to say they do something creative like throw pots or write poems.

Bishop: I just came back in March from reading in North Carolina and Arkansas, and I swear if I see any more handcrafts I'll go mad! I think we should go right straight back to the machine. You can only use so many leather belts, after all. I'm sorry. Maybe you do some of these things.

Interviewer: Do many strangers send you poems?

Bishop: Yes. It's very hard to know what to do. Sometimes I answer. I had a fan letter the other day, and it was adorable. It was in this childish handwriting. His name was Jimmy Sparks and he was in the sixth grade. He said his class was putting together a booklet of poems and he liked my poems very much—he mentioned three— because they rhymed and because they were about nature. His letter was so cute I did send him a postcard. I think he was supposed to ask me to send a handwritten poem or photograph—schools do this all the time—but he didn't say anything like that, and I'm sure he forgot his mission.

Interviewer: What three poems did he like? "The Sandpiper"?

Bishop: Yes, and the one about the mirror and the moon, "Insomnia," which Marianne Moore said was a cheap love poem.

Interviewer: The one that ends, ". . . and you love me"?

Bishop: Yes. I never liked that. I almost left it out. But last year it was put to music by Elliott Carter along with five other poems of mine* and it sounded much better as a song. Yes, Marianne was very opposed to that one.

---

*"Anaphora," "The Sandpiper," "Argument," "O Breath," and "View of the Capitol from The Library of Congress."

Interviewer: Maybe she didn't like the last line.

Bishop: I don't think she ever believed in talking about the emotions much.

Interviewer: Getting back to teaching, did you devise formal assignments when you taught at Harvard? For example, to write a villanelle?

Bishop: Yes, I made out a whole list of weekly assignments that I gave the class; but every two or three weeks was a free assignment and they could hand in what they wanted. Some classes were so prolific that I'd declare a moratorium. I'd say, "Please, nobody write a poem for two weeks!"

Interviewer: Do you think you can generalize that beginning writers write better in forms than not?

Bishop: I don't know. We did a sestina—we started one in class by drawing words out of a hat—and I wish I'd never suggested it because it seemed to have *swept* Harvard. Later, in the applications for my class, I'd get dozens of sestinas. The students seemed to think it was my favorite form—which it isn't.

Interviewer: I once tried a sestina about a woman who watches soap operas all day.

Bishop: Did you watch them in college?

Interviewer: No.

Bishop: Well, it seemed to be a fad at Harvard. Two or three years ago I taught a course in prose and discovered my students were watching the soap operas every morning and afternoon. I don't know when they studied. So I watched two or three just to see what was going on. They were *boring*. And the advertising! One student wrote a story about an old man who was getting ready to have an old lady to dinner (except she was really a ghost), and he polished a plate till he could see his face in it. It was quite well done, so I read some of it aloud, and said, "But look, this is impossible. You can never see your face in a plate." The whole class, in unison, said, "Joy!" I said, "What? What are you talking about?" Well, it seems there's an ad for Joy soap liquid in which a woman holds up a plate and sees—you know the one? Even so, you can't! I found this very disturbing. TV was *real* and no one had observed that it wasn't. Like when Aristotle was right and no one pointed out, for centuries, that women *don't* have fewer teeth then men.

I had a friend bring me a small TV, black and white, when I was

living in Brazil. We gave it to the maid almost immediately because
we only watched it when there were things like political speeches, or
a revolution coming on. But she loved it. She slept with it in her bed!
I think it meant so much to her because she couldn't read. There was
a soap opera that year called "The Right to Life." It changed the
whole schedule of Rio society's hours because it was on from eight to
nine. The usual dinner hour's eight, so either you had to eat dinner
before so that the maid could watch "The Right to Life" or eat much
later, when it was over. We ate dinner about ten o'clock finally so that
Joanna could watch this thing. I finally decided I had to see it, too. It
became a chic thing to do and everybody was taking about it. It was
absolutely ghastly! They got the programs from Mexico and dubbed
them in Portuguese. They were very corny and always very lurid.
Corpses lying in coffins, miracles, nuns, even incest.

I had friends in Belo Horizonte and the mother and their cook and
a grandchild would watch the soap operas, the *novellas,* they're
called, every night. The cook would get so excited she'd talk to the
screen: "No! No! Don't do that! You know he's a bad man, Dona So-
and-so!" They'd get so excited, they'd cry. And I knew of two old
ladies, sisters, who got a TV. They'd knit and knit and watch it and
cry and one of them would get up and say, "Excuse me, I have to go
to the bathroom," to the television!

Interviewer: You were living in Brazil, weren't you, when you won
the Pulitzer Prize in 1956?

Bishop: Yes, it was pretty funny. We lived on top of a mountain
peak—really way up in the air. I was alone in the house with Maria,
the cook. A friend had gone to market. The telephone rang. It was a
newsman from the American Embassy and he asked me who it was in
English, and of course it was very rare to hear someone speak in
English. He said, "Do you know you've won the Pulitzer Prize?"
Well, I thought it was a joke. I said, "Oh, come on." And he said,
"Don't you hear me?" The telephone connection was very bad and
he was shrieking. And I said, "Oh, it can't be." But he said it wasn't
a joke. I couldn't make an impression on Maria with this news, but I
felt I had to share it, so I hurried down the mountain a half mile or so
to the next house, but no one was at home. I thought I should do
something to celebrate, have a glass of wine or something. But all I
could find in that house, a friend's, were some cookies from America,

some awful chocolate cookies—Oreos, I think—so I ended up eating two of those. And that's how I celebrated winning the Pulitzer Prize.

The next day there was a picture in the afternoon paper—they take such things very seriously in Brazil—and the day after that my Brazilian friend went to market again. There was a big covered market with stalls for every kind of comestible, and there was one vegetable man we always went to. He said, "Wasn't that Dona Elizabetchy's picture in the paper yesterday?" She said, "Yes, it was. She won a prize." And he said, "You know, it's amazing! Last week Senhora (Somebody) took a chance on a bicycle and *she* won! My customers are so lucky!" Isn't that marvelous?!

Interviewer: I'd like to talk a little bit about your stories, especially "In the Village," which I've always admired. Do you see any connection, other than the obvious one of shared subject matter, between your stories and poems? In "method of attack," for example?

Bishop: They're very closely related. I suspect that some of the stories I've written are actually prose poems and not very good stories. I have four about Nova Scotia. One came out last year in the *Southern Review*. I'm working on a long one now that I hope to finish this summer. . . . "In the Village" was funny. I had made notes for various bits of it and was given too much cortisone—I have very bad asthma from time to time—and you don't need any sleep. You feel wonderful while it's going on, but to get off it is awful. So I couldn't sleep much and I sat up all night in the tropical heat. The story came from a combination of cortisone, I think, and the gin and tonic I drank in the middle of the night. I wrote it in two nights.

Interviewer: That's incredible! It's a long, long story.

Bishop: Extraordinary. I wish I could do it again but I'll never take cortisone again, if I can possibly avoid it.

Interviewer: I'm always interested in how different poets go about writing about their childhood.

Bishop: Everybody does. You can't help it, I suppose. You are fearfully observant then. You notice all kinds of things, but there's no way of putting them all together. My memories of some of those days are so much clearer than things that happened in 1950, say. I don't think one should make a cult of writing about childhood, however. I've always tried to avoid it. I find I have written some, I must say. I went to an analyst for a couple of years off and on in the forties, a very nice woman who was especially interested in writers, writers and blacks. She said it was amazing that I would remember things that happened to me when I was two. It's very rare, but apparently writers often do.

Interviewer: Do you know what your earliest memory is?

Bishop: I think I remember learning to walk. My mother was away and my grandmother was trying to encourage me to walk. It was in Canada and she had lots of plants in the window the way all ladies do there. I can remember this blur of plants and my grandmother holding out her arms. I must have toddled. It seems to me it's a memory. It's very hazy. I told my grandmother years and years later and she said, "Yes, you did learn to walk while your mother was visiting someone." But you walk when you're one, don't you?

I remember my mother taking me for a ride on the swan boats here in Boston. I think I was three then. It was before we went back to Canada. Mother was dressed all in black—widows were in those days. She had a box of mixed peanuts and raisins. There were real swans floating around. I don't think they have them anymore. A swan came up and she fed it and it bit her finger. Maybe she just told me this, but I believed it because she showed me her black kid glove and said, "See." The finger was split. Well, I was thrilled to death! Robert Lowell put those swan boats in two or three of the *Lord Weary's Castle* poems.

Interviewer: Your childhood was difficult, and yet in many of your stories and poems about that time there's a tremendously lyrical quality as well as a great sense of loss and tragedy.

Bishop: My father died, my mother went crazy when I was four or five years old. My relatives, I think they all felt so sorry for this child that they tried to do their very best. And I think they did. I lived with my grandparents in Nova Scotia. Then I lived with the ones in Worcester, Massachusetts, very briefly, and got terribly sick. This was when I was six and seven. Then I lived with my mother's older sister in Boston. I used to go to Nova Scotia for the summer. When I was twelve or thirteen I was improved enough to go to summer camp at Wellfleet until I went away to school when I was fifteen or sixteen. My aunt was devoted to me and she was awfully nice. She was married and had no children. But my relationship with my relatives—I was always a sort of a guest, and I think I've always felt like that.

Interviewer: Was your adolescence a calmer time?

Bishop: I was very romantic. I once walked from Nauset Light—I don't think it exists anymore—which is the beginning of the elbow [of Cape Cod], to the tip, Provincetown, all alone. It took me a night and a day. I went swimming from time to time but at that time the beach was absolutely deserted. There wasn't anything on the back shore, no buildings.

Interviewer: How old would you have been?

Bishop: Seventeen or eighteen. That's why I'd never go back—because I can't bear to think of the way it is now. . . . I haven't been to Nantucket since, well, I hate to say. My senior year at college I went there for Christmas with my then boyfriend. Nobody knew we were there. It was this wonderful, romantic trip. We went the day after Christmas and stayed for about a week. It was terribly cold but beautiful. We took long walks on the moors. We stayed at a very nice inn and we thought that probably the landlady would throw us out (we were very young and this kind of thing wasn't so common then). We had a bottle of sherry or something innocent like that. On New Year's Eve about ten o'clock there was a knock on the door. It was our landlady with a tray of hot grogs! She came in and we had the loveliest time. She knew the people who ran the museum and they opened it for us. There are a couple of wonderful museums there.

Interviewer: I heard a story that you once spent a night in a tree at Vassar outside Cushing dormitory. Is it true?

Bishop: Yes, it was me, me and a friend whose name I can't remember. We really were crazy and those trees were wonderful to climb. I used to be a great tree climber. Oh, we probably gave up about three in the morning. How did that ever get around? I can't imagine! We stopped being friends afterwards. Well, actually she had invited two boys from West Point for the weekend and I found myself *stuck* with this youth all in—[her hands draw an imagined cape and uniform in the air]—the dullest boy! I didn't know what to say! I nearly went mad. I think I sort of dropped the friend at that point. . . . I lived in a great big corner room on the top floor of Cushing and I apparently had registered a little late because I had a roommate whom I had never wanted to have. A strange girl named Constance. I remember her entire side of the room was furnished in Scotty dogs—pillows, pictures, engravings, and photographs. And mine was rather

bare. Except that I probably wasn't a good roommate either, because
I had a theory at that time that one should write down all one's
dreams. That that was the way to write poetry. So I kept a notebook
of my dreams and thought if you ate a lot of awful cheese at bedtime
you'd have interesting dreams. I went to Vassar with a pot about this
big—it did have a cover!—of Roquefort cheese that I kept in the
bottom of my bookcase. . . . I think everyone's given to eccentricities
at that age. I've heard that at Oxford Auden slept with a revolver
under his pillow.

Interviewer: As a young woman, did you have a sense of yourself
as a writer?

Bishop: No, it all just happens without your thinking about it. I
never meant to go to Brazil. I never meant doing any of these things.
I'm afraid in my life everything has just *happened.*

Interviewer: You like to think there are reasons—

Bishop: Yes, that people plan ahead, but I'm afraid I really didn't.

Interviewer: But you'd always been interested in writing?

Bishop: I'd written since I was a child but when I went to Vassar I
was going to be a composer. I'd studied music at Walnut Hill and had
a rather good teacher. I'd had a year of counterpoint and I also played
the piano. At Vassar you had to perform in public once a month. Well,
this terrified me. I really was sick. So I played once and then I gave
up the piano because I couldn't bear it. I don't think I'd mind now,
but I can't play the piano anymore. Then the next year I switched
to English.

It was a very literary class. Mary McCarthy was a year ahead of
me. Eleanor Clark was in my class. And Muriel Rukeyser, for fresh-
man year. We started a magazine you may have heard of, *Con Spirito.*
I think I was a junior then. There were six or seven of us—Mary,
Eleanor Clark and her older sister, my friends Margaret Miller and
Frani Blough, and a couple of others. It was during Prohibition and
we used to go downtown to a speakeasy and drink wine out of
teacups. That was our big vice. Ghastly stuff! Most of us had submitted things to the *Vassar Review* and they'd been turned down. It was
very old-fashioned then. We were all rather put out because *we*
thought we were good. So we thought, Well, we'll start our own
magazine. We thought it would be nice to have it anonymous, which
it was. After its third issue the *Vassar Review* came around and a

couple of our editors became editors on it and then they published things by us. But we had a wonderful time doing it while it lasted.

Interviewer: I read in another interview you gave that you had enrolled or were ready to enroll after college in Cornell Medical School.

Bishop: I think I had all the forms. This was the year after I had graduated from Vassar. But then I discovered I would have to take German and I'd already given up on German once, I thought it was so difficult. And I would have had to take another year of chemistry. I'd already published a few things and I think Marianne [Moore] discouraged me, and I didn't go. I just went off to Europe instead.

Interviewer: Did the Depression have much reality for college students in the thirties?

Bishop: Everybody was frantic trying to get jobs. All the intellectuals were Communist except me. I'm always very perverse so I went in for T. S. Eliot and Anglo-Catholicism. But the spirit was pretty radical. It's funny. The girl who was the biggest radical—she was a year ahead of me—has been married for years and years to one of the heads of Time-Life. I've forgotten his name. He's very famous and couldn't be more conservative. He writes shocking editorials. I can still see her standing outside the library with a tambourine collecting money for this cause and that cause.

Interviewer: Wanting to be a composer, a doctor, or a writer—how do you account for it?

Bishop: Oh, I was interested in all those things. I'd like to be a painter most, I think. I never really sat down and said to myself, "I'm going to be a poet." Never in my life. I'm still surprised that people think I am. . . . I started publishing things in my senior year, I think, and I remember my first check for thirty-five dollars and that was rather an exciting moment. It was from something called *The Magazine,* published in California. They took a poem, they took a story—oh, I wish those poems had never been published! They're terrible! I did show the check to my roommate. I was on the newspaper, *The Miscellany*—and I really was, I don't know, mysterious. On the newspaper board they used to sit around and talk about how they could get published and so on and so on. I'd just hold my tongue. I was embarrassed by it. And still am. There's nothing more embarrassing than being a poet, really.

Interviewer: It's especially difficult to tell people you're meeting for the first time that that's what you do.

Bishop: Just last week a friend and I went to visit a wonderful lady I know in Quebec. She's seventy-four or seventy-five. And she didn't say this to me but she said to my friend, Alice, "I'd like to ask my neighbor who has the big house next door to dinner, and she's so nice, but she'd be bound to ask Elizabeth what she does and if Elizabeth said she wrote poetry, the poor woman wouldn't say another word all evening!" This is awful, you know, and I think no matter how modest you think you feel or how minor you think you are, there must be an awful core of ego somewhere for you to set yourself up to write poetry. I've never *felt* it, but it must be there.

Interviewer: In your letter to me, you sounded rather wary of interviewers. Do you feel you've been misrepresented in interviews? For example, that your refusal to appear in all-women poetry anthologies has been misunderstood as a kind of disapproval of the feminist movement.

Bishop: I've always considered myself a strong feminist. Recently I was interviewed by a reporter from *The Chicago Tribune*. After I talked to the girl for a few minutes, I realized that she wanted to play me off as an "old-fashioned" against Erica Jong, and Adrienne [Rich], whom I like, and other violently feminist people. Which isn't true at all. I finally asked her if she'd ever read any of my poems. Well, it seemed she'd read *one* poem. I didn't see how she could interview me if she didn't know anything about me at all, and I told her so. She was nice enough to print a separate piece in *The Chicago Tribune* apart from the longer article on the others. I had said that I didn't believe in propaganda in poetry. That it rarely worked. What she had me saying was, "Miss Bishop does not believe that poetry should convey the poet's personal philosophy." Which made me sound like a complete dumbbell! Where she got that, I don't know. This is why one gets nervous about interviews.

Interviewer: Do you generally agree with anthologists' choices? Do you have any poems that are personal favorites? Ones you'd like to see anthologized that aren't?

Bishop: I'd rather have—well, anything except "The Fish"! I've declared a moratorium on that. Anthologists repeat each other so finally a few years ago I said nobody could reprint "The Fish" unless they reprinted three others because I got so sick of it.

Interviewer: One or two more questions. You went to Yaddo several times early in your career. Did you find the atmosphere at an artist's colony helpful to your writing?

Bishop: I went to Yaddo twice, once in the summer for two weeks, and for several months the winter before I went to Brazil. Mrs. Ames was very much in evidence then. I didn't like it in the summer because of the incessant coming and going, but the winter was rather different. There were only six of us and just by luck we all liked each other and had a very good time. I wrote one poem, I think, in that whole stretch. The first time I liked the horse races, I'm afraid. In the summer—I think this still goes on—you can walk through the Whitney estate to the tracks. A friend and I used to walk there early in the morning and sit at the track and have coffee and blueberry muffins while they exercised the horses. I loved that. We went to a sale of yearlings in August and that was beautiful. The sale was in a big tent. The grooms had brass dustpans and brooms with brass handles and they'd go around after the little colts and sweep up the manure. That's what I remember best about Yaddo.

Interviewer: It was around the time that you went to Yaddo, wasn't it, that you were consultant in poetry to the Library of Congress? Was that year in Washington more productive than your Yaddo experience?

Bishop: I've suffered because I've been so shy all my life. A few years later I might have enjoyed it more but at the time I didn't like it much. I hated Washington. There were so many government buildings that looked like Moscow. There was a very nice secretary, Phyllis Armstrong, who got me through. I think she did most of the work. I'd write something and she'd say, "Oh, no, that isn't official," so then she'd take it and rewrite it in gobbledegook. We used to bet on the horses—Phyllis always bet the daily double. She and I would sit there reading the *Racing Form* and poets would come to call and Phyllis and I would be talking about our bets!

All the "survivors" of that job—a lot of them are dead—were invited to read there recently. There were thirteen of us, unfortunately.

Interviewer: A friend of mine tried to get into that reading and she said it was jammed.

Bishop: It was *mobbed!* And I don't know why. It couldn't have been a duller, more awful occasion. I think we were supposedly limited to ten minutes. I *stuck* to it. But there's no stopping somebody like James Dickey. Stafford was good. I'd never heard him and never met him. He read one very short poem that really brought tears to my eyes, he read it so beautifully.

I'm not very fond of poetry readings. I'd much rather read the book. I know I'm wrong. I've only been to a few poetry readings I could *bear.* Of course, you're too young to have gone through the Dylan Thomas craze. . . .

When it was somebody like Cal Lowell or Marianne Moore, it's as if they were my children. I'd get terribly upset. I went to hear Marianne several times and finally I just couldn't go because I'd sit there with tears running down my face. I don't know, it's sort of embarrassing. You're so afraid they'll do something wrong.

Cal thought that the most important thing about readings was the remarks poets made in between the poems. The first time I heard him read was years ago at the New School for Social Research in a small, gray auditorium. It was with Allen Tate and Louise Bogan. Cal was very much younger than anybody else and had published just two books. He read a long, endless poem—I've forgotten its title*—about a Canadian nun in New Brunswick. I've forgotten what the point of the poem is, but it's very, very long and it's quite beautiful, particularly in the beginning. Well, he started, and he read very badly. He kind of droned and everybody was trying to get it. He had gotten about two-thirds of the way through when somebody yelled, "Fire!" There was a small fire in the lobby, nothing much, that was put out in about five minutes and everybody went back to their seats. Poor Cal said, "I think I'd better begin over again," so he read the whole thing all over again! But his reading got much, much better in later years.

Interviewer: He couldn't have done any better than the record the Poetry Center recently put out. It's wonderful. And very funny.

Bishop: I haven't the courage to hear it.

---

*"Mother Marie Therese" in *The Mills of the Kavanaughs.*

Elizabeth Bishop's Library: A Reminiscence

Mildred J. Nash / 1983

Reprinted from the *Massachusetts Review*, 24 (Summer 1983), 433–37. Copyright © 1984 The Massachusetts Review, Inc.

I have stopped wondering, now, and simply accept my good fortune at having been chosen by Elizabeth Bishop to take part in her writing workshop in the fall of 1976. Elizabeth Bishop was one of Harvard's triumvirate of poets, then; the other two were Robert Lowell and Robert Fitzgerald. When I saw my name posted on Miss Bishop's list (this was before I'd considered that we might move to first names later) I could hardly believe it. That we might become friends seemed equally unlikely.

In retrospect, I am still unable to explain why she chose me for such an honor. Several times she had marveled that someone from the Harvard Ed School could write without a trace of the educational jargon she despised. Once she confided that I was the only Harvard student she had ever had who turned all work in on time. (I never felt quite comfortable with that compliment; who, after all, wants to be un-Harvardian?) And yet I suspected that Miss Bishop felt as little at home at Harvard as I did. In any event, she was facing mandatory retirement at 65 that spring. Perhaps Miss Bishop simply noticed my being older than the others in the group. After all, no one else had showed up on a ''snow day'' with an eight year old daughter in tow. In fact, that was the first time Miss Bishop invited me (daughter and all!) to join her for coffee at Piroschka's, a treat we repeated several times before the school year ended.

After Harvard, I hadn't the courage to telephone Miss Bishop, even though she had made a great point of giving me her unlisted number. In the autumn of 1977, when I needed a recommendation, I wrote to her. The next day my phone rang—Miss Bishop wanted me to come to her place with the necessary forms—and, of course, my daughters were welcome too! Our occasional phone calls and visits had begun.

Then, late in 1978, Elizabeth (by now she had insisted that I use her
first name) phoned to see if I might have time to help her re-arrange
her library. I leaped at the chance. One tall wall of each of her
spacious Lewis Wharf rooms (the kitchen was hardly room-size) was
lined with shelves which towered twice her height. They were
crowded with titles I had glanced at and wondered about each time I
had visited. Talk of pay was quickly turned to more agreeable terms:
I could have first crack at her discards and duplicates, and she was
willing to wait until I had time to tackle the task during my winter vacation.

We began with the travel section. It was to the right of the living
room window that, descending from the ceiling almost to the floor,
overlooked Boston Harbor. I kept one eye out for exotic ships. So
did Elizabeth. A strange flag—or even a familiar but unusual one—
would send her scurrying for binoculars and a worn copy of *The
Observers' Book of Flags*. Her fascination with travel showed also in
the assortment of countries I found myself trying to arrange alphabeti-
cally by continent. Many of the books were about Brazil. My questions about places I had never heard of led us to the coffee table to
look at the large world atlas, a Christmas gift she had long wanted and
just the past year received.

Practically all the rest of the living room wall except for the
especially tall bottom shelf on which she kept her art books—a twenty
foot row of them—and a six foot section of philosophy, was reserved
for novels. She had most of the expected classics and many thick,
unfamiliar volumes, but no very recent bestsellers, so far as I can
recall. Almost swallowed up among these collections were a foot and
a half of psychology books, six inches of Octavio Paz (whom she
dearly loved, she said, but didn't understand), and two feet of cookbooks.

Work on any row of books invariably led to a discussion of the
genre. By purest accident, I am sure, while we were discussing
cookbooks, we were interrupted by a phone call. A friend asked for
her recipe for lobster chowder. That reminded her of another telephone request; once the president of Bryn Mawr had called to get the
recipe for a fish chowder which Elizabeth had served the evening
before. In fact, the chowder had been bought at the Boston Fish
Pier's famous No Name Restaurant. But she faked a recipe nonethe-

less, and I'd like to think that her august caller was not hurt at all by the deception.

No sooner had I finished the cookbook section than Elizabeth put lunch on the tiny table which occupied the kitchen-side corner of her living room. The omelet was accompanied by tasty smoked ham from Arkansas ("The only good thing in that state," Elizabeth volunteered, although I afterward learned that she was also very impressed by the creative writing students at the University of Arkansas.)

Our progress through the books was slow, continually interrupted by Elizabeth's fascinating detours into barely related or unrelated areas. In an early, seemingly endless poetry reading by Robert Lowell, he was halfway through a long poem when smoke and a yell of "Fire!" emptied the auditorium. After the listeners faithfully returned, they greeted with a groan his words, "I think I should start over." Elizabeth admitted that she hated to go to readings as much as she hated to give them. . . . Binoculars in use again, she inquired if those could be scaup in the harbor. "What do they eat in that polluted water?" . . . Did I ever send to *The New Yorker?* There one got a fair reading—she had Howard Moss's assurance and she trusted him one hundred per cent—well, almost one hundred per cent. . . . Could I believe that she had spent five days preparing a talk on translation and then found that the B.U. professor who had asked her for it thought she had turned him down and so had not included a place for her on the schedule? . . . She warned me not to heed reviewers—only one had ever said what she would say about her work. He was a sweet Englishman who had written anonymously. Later she had visited his house—on the very day he had buried his wife. Although she felt dreadful going through with an invitation at such a sad time, he had been wonderfully thoughtful. . . .

I was able to make progress on the book arrangement only when Elizabeth zipped into a ski jacket and went off to buy *The New York Times,* clear up a bouncing check at the bank, and collect her mail (a letter from *Harper's* wanting essays "to order," "the lowest phone bill in years," and news from her lawyer about mudslides in the area around her Brazilian home which dated from the 1600s). The Brazilian disaster caused us to stop again, this time to look at photographs of Elizabeth's South American house. She told about the time there when she had noticed a snake slithering along the edge of the dining room floor as she was serving lunch to an American friend. Hoping that her friend wouldn't notice, Elizabeth calmly suggested that they move into the living room for dessert. Once her entertaining was over, she searched and searched for that snake, which she never did find.

Occasionally Elizabeth would disappear into her study for a bit of quick typing, but it was hard for her to abandon the dusty books which triggered her asthma as well as her curiosity. Many books had an additional irritant, a white, powdery insecticide sprinkled into the pages when her Brazilian library became threatened by some paper-eating insects. Their tunnels were still evident in many a book.

We took a coffee break. As she poured herself one more cup than her doctor recommended, she discussed the medical world's disagreement about coffee's effect on hernias.

She talked of marriage for love as a new and western invention. "It just never worked out for me, but I don't regret—all things considered—its not happening," she said. Of mothers she remarked that from all she had seen and heard of her friends' mothers, she was probably just as well off without one.

All of a sudden she felt feminist outrage at being told twice the day before that she looked like "anyone's grandmother" or "someone's great aunt." "Robert Fitzgerald's older than I and no one tells him, 'You look like anyone's grandfather.' "

Wondering why I wanted to teach when I didn't need the money, Elizabeth told how she had quickly recovered from the feeling that one ought to work. Fresh from college she had taken a job writing (under the pseudonym Mr. Something-or-other) for a rather shady firm. Unable to tolerate the position, she had quit shortly before all the company's employees were arrested for mail fraud. Thereafter she was able for many years to live frugally on her father's inheritance, supplemented by checks from her writing.

We spent a good deal of time searching unsuccessfully for a phonograph record of Brazilian bird songs. Remembering Lowell's visit to Brazil, Elizabeth laughed, "Only the gaudy birds kept Cal from going crazy with boredom." Then we were side-tracked by her photo albums. One was filled with French movie stars, the mistresses of rich Brazilians; the other was of relatives (labelled mainly "unknown relatives") and some baby pictures ("I was at my loveliest at nine months").

In her study Elizabeth's best books—dictionaries, rhyming dictionaries, George Herbert, an annotated edition of the Opies' *Nursery
Rhyme Book* (how I wished they had needed dusting so I could have
examined those titles more closely)—were on a multi-layered circular
bookcase placed right next to her desk.

The study's book wall was mainly poetry, except for the bottom
two shelves on which rested her Spanish and Portuguese collection,
plus some French books. I especially envied the many-volume, blue-
covered set of Fabre's *Souvenirs entomologiques,* an inheritance from
a relative. Her heavily written-in Greek texts too were here. "My
college grades suffered from my prolonged failure to learn Greek."
Evidently algebra had been even more of a nemesis: "I was so bad I
broke all college board records for low scores. I got a 2, I think. At
any rate, I had to wait a year to enter college because of that."

As we sorted through the poetry books, Elizabeth reminisced. One
book caused her to exclaim, "He was the only student I ever kicked
out of class, but he wouldn't stop talking—and now he even has a
poem in here for me!"

Significantly missing among her library holdings were books of
criticism, an area for which she seemed to have little use. The few
such books she kept, written by friends, were tucked in among their
authors' more respectable volumes of poetry and fiction.

Three leisurely days' work had left us with still one room to go.
That, however, had to wait until my April vacation when finally we
arrived at the bedroom wall of books, the inner sanctum of her library.
Here she kept some of her best treasures: her field guides to birds,
wildflowers, seashores, rocks, and the like. Almost all of Beatrix
Potter's volumes were lined up beside interesting South American
artifacts and toys, as were several other sets of small poetry volumes.
Old art magazines were stacked on the bottom shelves—to be dis-
posed of, although Elizabeth could never quite carry out the final
disposition. Someone must want them, she was sure. Here were
biographies galore, a full shelf and a half from ceiling almost to floor.
Lewis Carroll had two biographies, as did Edward Lear. How she
adored that man! She paused to leaf through his *Nonsense Book,*
talking of his sad life.

Apologizing for the rheumatism which kept her from getting down
to inspect the bottom shelf, Elizabeth stood while I handed her the

accumulated piles of periodicals, one of which triggered her profound annoyance. She had been interviewed in the same *Vassar Quarterly* issue as had Muriel Rukeyser. "I sound so frivolous beside her—I chatting of this and that while she tells of front line Korea and such.' . . . And she mentions me while I never mention her.''

There were photographs of her Brazilian companion, Lota de Macedo Soares, and of the toucan whose death she felt responsible for and could not bear to discuss. There was a book set out on her bed because it was so full of good words that she planned to make a poem of them. (I wished I had the audacity to stop and see what book it was.) There was a book of John Skelton's poems set out because one poem in it had set Elizabeth off on a poem of her own. There were her friends' latest publications—and Flannery O'Connor's *Letters* which she was enjoying at the moment.

Our last day of work was almost over before I could summon sufficient courage to ask the question which had been on the tip of my tongue ever since I had attended Miss Bishop's Harvard classes. In an embarrassed rush I confessed that I had long wondered why her next-to-present book was titled *The Complete Poems*. Turning away as she spoke, Elizabeth gave an amazingly simple explanation: she had been living in Brazil at the time, and in the back and forth shuffle of galley mailings to New York, she had somehow overlooked the erroneous title page proofs for her collected poems.

After four long but fast-passing days, the task was finished. Elizabeth declared happily that her library was set for another four years. I had happily hauled to my car nine shopping bags of books including Elizabeth's second rhyming dictionary, well-worn duplicate copies of Yeats's and Auden's *Collected Poems,* a duplicate Lear biography, an alpine flower book, a tropical bird book, an autographed copy of Elizabeth's *Complete Poems,* a left-handed can-opener and a cache of candy for my daughters—plus two large pink cans of a special Texas brand of grapefruit juice from the two cartons which she and her friend Alice Methfessel had bought to take to Maine for the summer.

Somehow Elizabeth seemed to feel that she couldn't thank me enough for what I regarded as one of my most memorable opportunities. But of course there's no way I can thank her enough either.

Studying with Miss Bishop
Dana Gioia / 1986

Reprinted by permission; © 1986 Dana Gioia. Originally in the
New Yorker, 15 September 1986, 90–101.

In February, 1975, I began my last semester as a graduate student in
English at Harvard University. Picking my courses that final term, I
tried for once to pick them carefully, and I came down to a choice
between two teachers—Robert Lowell and Elizabeth Bishop. Mr.
Lowell's seminar on nineteenth-century poets was very popular.
Everyone who fancied himself a poet talked about taking it. As for
Elizabeth Bishop's course on modern poetry, I had never heard
anyone mention it at all. It seemed to exist only in the course
catalogue: "English 285: Studies in Modern Poetry: Miss Elizabeth
Bishop, Instructor."

In retrospect, one might imagine that it would have been nearly
impossible to get into one of Elizabeth Bishop's classes. But this was
not the case. Her course was not one of the many that Harvard
students fought to get into and afterward always managed to mention
they had taken. The most popular teachers among the young literary
elite were Robert Lowell, William Alfred, Robert Fitzgerald, and the
newly arrived Alexander Theroux. On the first day of their classes, it
was difficult just to squeeze into the room. While Northrop Frye, who
was visiting Harvard that year to deliver the Norton Lectures, drew
audiences of nearly a thousand for his class on myth and literature,
Miss Bishop, I was to learn, rarely attracted more than a dozen
unenthusiastic undergraduates. Her manner was at odds with the
academic glamour of Harvard, her conversation not designed to
impress. She was a politely formal, shy, and undramatic woman. She
wanted no worshipful circle of students, and got none. Only her
writing course was popular, but all writing courses were in great
demand at Harvard, since the university as a matter of policy offered
very few. While the Cambridge literary establishment held Miss
Bishop in the highest esteem, among the undergraduates she was just
another writer on the faculty. They knew she was well known, but
wasn't everyone who taught at Harvard?

139

Miss Bishop's first session was held in a classroom on the second floor of Sever Hall, a grimy building of supposed architectural distinction in the Harvard Yard. The classroom—narrow, poorly whitewashed, with high, cracked ceilings—looked as if it belonged in an abandoned high school in North Dakota. There were exposed radiator pipes with peeling paint. A few battered shelves were lined with broken-spined textbooks of incalculable age. A couple of dozen chairs, no two of them matching, were set randomly around a huge, scratched table, at one end of which—prim, impeccably coiffured, and smoking—sat Miss Elizabeth Bishop.

I recognized her immediately from photographs I had seen in books, but somehow, suddenly coming into a room where she was sitting a few feet away, I was taken by surprise. At that point in my life, I had seen so few real poets in person that I felt a strange shock at being in the same room as someone whose work I knew on the page. It was an odd, almost uncomfortable sensation to have the perfect world of books peer so casually into the disorder of everyday life. I was also surprised by her appearance. She seemed disappointingly normal. I don't know exactly what I had expected—perhaps someone slightly bohemian or noticeably eccentric, a Marianne Moore or a Margaret Rutherford. Instead, I saw a very attractive woman in what I guessed to be her middle fifties (actually, she was sixty-four), dressed in a tasteful, expensive-looking suit, perfectly poised, waiting to begin. By the time the class started, only about a dozen students had arrived. I was surprised at so small a turnout. Moreover, we sat scattered around the room in a way that made the class seem half empty rather than intimate.

Eventually, she began. "I am Elizabeth Bishop," she announced, "and this is Studies in Modern Poetry. The way I usually run this class is by asking the students to choose three or four poets they would like to read and talk about. Does anyone have a suggestion?"

The first question was always an important moment in a Harvard class. It set the tone of the session, like the opening bid on the New York Stock Exchange.

"Can we read John Ashbery? Something like 'Self-Portrait in a Convex Mirror'?" a young man asked from the back of the room.

Now, this was a truly exceptional question. Ashbery was just becoming well known, and every young poet I knew had been reading him. But hardly anyone was able to understand Ashbery. His work was so elusive and difficult that people who talked authoritatively about it were held in universally high regard.

"Ashbery?" said Miss Bishop. "Oh, no, we can't read Ashbery. I wouldn't know what to say about him."

"Couldn't we try an early book?" the student said.

"No, no. Let's try someone else."

"What about Auden?" another student asked.

"Oh, I love Auden, but we can't do him."

"Why not?"

"We just read him in my other class. We should read new people."

She acted as if we knew exactly what authors she had assigned the previous semester. I felt at ease. At least she was disorganized. I didn't have to revise my stereotype of poets entirely.

That first session must have seemed particularly unpromising. By the second class, the dozen original students had dwindled down to five—four undergraduates and me. The administration responded by moving us into a more intimate facility—the "seminar room" in the basement of Kirkland House. One entered by finding a well-hidden side door in one of the dormitory's wings, descending several staircases, and then wandering about until one came upon a vast, colorless room full of unwanted furniture and dismembered bicycles. There were pipes on the ceiling, and an endless Ping-Pong game went on behind a thin partition. In one corner stood a table slightly larger than a card table, and that was the only usable table in the place. Eventually, we all found the room, and the six of us took our places facing one another across the tiny surface.

"I'm not a very good teacher," Miss Bishop began. "So to make sure you learn something in this class I am going to ask each of you to memorize at least ten lines a week from one of the poets we are reading." Had she announced that we were all required to attend class in sackcloth and ashes, the undergraduates could not have looked more horrified. This was the twentieth century, the age of criticism.

"Memorize poems?" someone asked. "But why?"

"So that you'll learn something in spite of me."

People exchanged knowing glances, as if to say, "We're dealing with a real oddball." But the subject was closed.

Her modesty was entirely sincere. She was the most self-effacing writer I have ever met. She had her own opinions and preferences, but there was no false pride in her. Several times in almost every class, she would throw up her hands and say, "I have no idea what this line means. Can anybody figure it out?" And all of us would then scuffle ineffectually to her rescue.

Teaching did not come naturally to her. She was almost sixty when she became an instructor at Harvard, and one could sense how uneasy she felt in the role. She would not lecture to us, even informally. Sessions with her were not so much classes as conversations. She would ask someone to read a poem aloud. If it was a long poem, then each of us would read a stanza in turn. (At times, it reminded me of a reading class in grammar school.) Then we would talk about the poem line by line in a relaxed, unorganized way. She rarely made an attempt to summarize any observations at the end of discussions. She enjoyed pointing out the particulars of each poem, not generalizing about it, and she insisted that we understand every individual word, even if we had no idea what the poem was about as a whole. "Use the dictionary," she said once. "It's better than the critics."

She had no system in approaching poems, and her practice of close reading had little in common with the disciplines of New Criticism. She did not attempt to tie the details of a poem together into a tight structure. She would have found that notion unappealing. Nor did she see poems in any strict historical perspective. Good poems existed for her in a sort of eternal present. Studying poetry with her was a leisurely process. The order of the words in the poem was the only agenda, and we would go from word to word, from line to line, as if we had all the time in the world. We only read poems she liked, and it was a pleasure at Harvard to have a teacher who, however baffled she might be in managing her class, clearly enjoyed the things she was talking about.

We began with poems from *Spring and All,* by William Carlos Williams. We worked through each poem as slowly as if it had been written in a foreign language, and Miss Bishop provided a detailed commentary: biographical information, publication dates, geographical facts, and personal anecdotes about her meetings with the poet.

She particularly admired the passage with which Williams opened the title poem of *Spring and All:*

> By the road to the contagious hospital
> under the surge of the blue
> mottled clouds driven from the
> northeast—a cold wind. Beyond, the
> waste of broad, muddy fields
> brown with dried weeds, standing and fallen
>
> patches of standing water
> the scattering of tall trees
>
> All along the road the reddish
> purplish, forked, upstanding, twiggy
> stuff of bushes and small trees
> with dead, brown leaves under them
> leafless vines

It took us about an hour to work through this straightforward passage, not because Miss Bishop had any thesis to prove but because it reminded her of so many things—wildflowers, New Jersey, the medical profession, modern painting. Her remarks often went beyond the point at hand, but frequently she made some phrase or passage we might have overlooked in the poem come alive through a brilliant, unexpected observation. For example, later in the poem Williams has four lines about plants coming up in the early spring:

> They enter the new world naked,
> cold, uncertain of all
> save that they enter. All about them
> the cold, familiar wind

"Williams is using a human metaphor for the plants," Miss Bishop explained. "As a doctor, he specialized in obstetrics, and here he sees the plants as if they were babies being born."

The poem of Williams' that she enjoyed talking about most was "The Sea-Elephant," which begins:

> Trundled from
> the strangeness of the sea—
> a kind of
> heaven—

> Ladies and Gentlemen!
> the greatest
> sea-monster ever exhibited
> alive
>
> the gigantic
> sea-elephant! O wallow
> of flesh where
> are
>
> there fish enough for
> that
> appetite stupidity
> cannot lessen?

One thing she found particularly fascinating about the poem was the way Williams made transitions. The poem moves quickly from one voice to the next, from one mood to another. It switches effortlessly from wonder to pathos, then to burlesque, and then back to wonder. I think this was the side of Williams' work closest to Bishop's own poetry. She, too, was a master of swift, unexpected transitions, and her poems move as surprisingly from amusement to wonder, from quiet pathos to joy. But with "The Sea-Elephant" the subject alone was enough to light up her interest. She loved talking about exotic animals or flowers, and, not surprisingly, she proved formidably well informed about sea elephants. And she admitted that for her the high point of the poem was the word that Williams invented to imitate the sea elephant's roar: "Blouaugh." It was music to her ears.

We began reading Wallace Stevens' work, and started with "The Man on the Dump." Here, too, I think the choice was revealing. She often named the poets who influenced her most as George Herbert, Gerard Manley Hopkins, Marianne Moore, and Stevens, and a poem like "The Man on the Dump" represents the side of Stevens' work most like her own. While the poem is pure Stevens in its central concerns, it is slightly uncharacteristic in style. The rhythms are freer and more unpredictable than the blank-verse poems it superficially resembles. The tone is wry and quiet, the organization smooth and conversational, not pseudodramatic. The catalogues of rubbish and flowers it contains are more typical of Bishop than of Stevens:

> Days pass like papers from a press.
> The bouquets come here in the papers.

> So the sun,
> And so the moon, both come, and the
> janitor's poems
> Of every day, the wrapper on the can
> of pears,
> The cat in the paper-bag, the corset,
> the box
> From Esthonia: the tiger chest, for tea.

Miss Bishop was more interested in Stevens' music than his philosophy, and she became most animated in discussing poems that bordered on inspired nonsense verse, where meaning was secondary to sound. She not only felt uncomfortable analyzing Stevens' ideas, she didn't even enjoy his more abstract works. Paging through Stevens' *Collected Poems* one afternoon, trying to figure out the next week's reading list, she claimed she wouldn't assign us a long, speculative poem, "The Comedian as the Letter C," because she couldn't stand to read it another time.

The only poem she specifically ordered us to memorize was Stevens' "The Emperor of Ice-Cream," and the next week she sat patiently through five stumbling recitations before leading us into a long discussion. Characteristically, she wanted us to memorize the poem before we talked about its meaning. To her, the images and the music of the lines were primary. If we comprehended the sound, eventually we would understand the sense. I also suspect that she stressed memorization in her class because it was one of the ways she herself approached poems. She knew dozens of Stevens' poems by heart and would quote them casually in conversation. She recited them like universally known maxims any of us might have brought up had we only thought of them first. Once, during a conversation on how Stevens used flowers, her face suddenly brightened and she said:

> There are no bears among the roses,
> Only a negress who supposes
> Things false and wrong
>
> About the lantern of the beauty
> Who walks there, as a farewell duty,
> Walks long and long.
>
> The pity that her pious egress
> Should fill the vigil of a negress
> With heat so strong!

It was a moment of joy. Catching us all by surprise, the poem left
us with the feeling of wonder that poetry should but so rarely is
allowed to evoke. The conversation stopped, and we all sat around
the table smiling like idiots. Miss Bishop was delighted at our reaction
but also shocked to learn that none of us knew the poem. (She was
always genuinely shocked to find that we did not know as much as
she did about poetry.) Someone asked the title of the poem. "I don't
know!" she exclaimed. " 'Bears and Roses,' I think." And then we
all began paging through our books in search of it. Eventually, we
found it—"The Virgin Carrying a Lantern."

To Miss Bishop, Stevens' greatest subject was not poetry, the
supreme fiction. It was Florida, the supreme landscape. She introduced us to Stevens with a long discourse on Florida—"the state with
the prettiest name," she said—and returned to the subject repeatedly,
always with affection and enthusiasm. But in a strange way her
memories of Florida had become as Platonic an ideal as Stevens'
visions of order at Key West. She was painfully aware of how much
of *her* Florida had vanished. Her comments on Key West were always
prefaced with disclaimers like "Back in the thirties, there used to be
. . . " She spoke of it as if she were Eve remembering Eden.

"More delicate than the historians' are the map-makers' colors,"
she once wrote, and, appropriately, she began her discussion of Key
West with a topographical fact. "Key West," she told us, "is only
ninety miles from Cuba." (Writing this down in my classroom notes,
I, who had never been south of Washington, D.C., had marvelous
visions of the Old South slipping mysteriously into Latin America in
landscapes framed by Spanish moss.) Later, in discussing "The
Emperor of Ice-Cream," she explained, "In the Depression, the town
was one-third Cuban, one-third black, and one-third everything else."
There were labor troubles, too, she said, and the cigar factories
moved to Tampa. The town was full of unemployed cigar rollers.
Cubans sold ice cream on the streets. People still used oil lamps. The
poem was inspired, she maintained, by a funeral Stevens saw in Key
West. Her explanation was the very antithesis of New Criticism. It
was, in fact, the very stuff of apocrypha, but she convinced me.

She also told us in detail how Stevens went to Key West every
winter with his friend and business associate Judge Arthur Powell.
She even knew the hotel they stayed at—the Casa Marina. Much to

our delight, she also told us, in disapproving tones, how, in 1936, Ernest Hemingway had beaten up Wallace Stevens once in Key West. It was, she informed us, Stevens' fault. He was drunk and had come up to Hemingway's wife (and Miss Bishop's friend), Pauline, and made an insulting comment about her clothes, which, we were further informed, "were perfectly respectable for a resort." Hemingway knocked Stevens flat. Miss Bishop spoke of the incident authoritatively and in great detail, as if she had been present. Perhaps she had. I later checked up on the incident, which seemed too colorful to be true, and found that it had really happened, though not exactly the way she described it. Stevens had actually insulted Pauline's sister, Ursula.

Miss Bishop disliked literary criticism. In 1950, she wrote for John Ciardi's anthology *Mid-Century American Poets:*

> The analysis of poetry is growing more and more pretentious and deadly. After a session with a few of the highbrow magazines one doesn't want to look at a poem for weeks, much less start writing one. . . . This does not mean that I am opposed to all close analysis and criticism. But I am opposed to making poetry monstrous or boring and proceeding to talk the very life out of it.

Twenty-five years later, her attitudes had only hardened on this subject. New Criticism was not only boring but misleading. She felt that most criticism reduced poems to ideas, and that the splendid particularity of an individual poem got lost in the process. A poem (if it was any good) could speak for itself. When she criticized the critics, she never spoke abstractly of "literary criticism," as if it were some branch of knowledge. Instead, she personalized the nemesis by referring collectively to "the critics," a sort of fumbling conspiracy of well-meaning idiots with access to printing presses. "They" were always mentioned in a kindly, disparaging way and dismissed with a single, elegant flip of her cigarette-holding hand.

Not dogmatic about her own theories, Miss Bishop did make a few exceptions: there were critics whom we were allowed to read without danger. "Allowed," however, is too weak a word, because when she liked a critic's work she liked it as intensely as the poems it talked about. Her favorite critic was her friend Randall Jarrell, who had been dead then for nearly ten years. His loss still seemed fresh, for she always spoke of him elegiacally, as if he had died only a few weeks before. Another critic she liked was Helen Vendler. She used Vendler's book *On Extended Wings,* about Stevens' longer poems, as a sort of Bible. Whenever we were to discuss one of the longer poems, she would bring Vendler's book to class. We would talk about the poem until the discussion reached an impasse, at which point Miss Bishop would suggest, "Now let's see what Vendler says." She would find chapter and verse, quote it, and only then let us go on.

I remember one rainy afternoon when a flu epidemic had decimated Cambridge. Only one other student besides me showed up for class, and the three of us sat around the table in the gloomy underworld of Kirkland House talking about "The Man with the Blue Guitar" and hearing the rain splatter against the basement windows. All of us were coughing from recent bouts with the flu, and especially Miss Bishop, who would still not stop smoking. She had, of course, brought her copy of *On Extended Wings,* and every few minutes she would stop the conversation to consult it. We would lean forward and wait for her to find the passage she wanted. Had a stranger suddenly been transported into the room, he would hardly have thought this was a seminar at Harvard University. It looked more like three old people in a rest home playing bridge with a dummy hand.

After Stevens, we moved on to Robert Lowell, and this switch gave us students an odd feeling of dislocation. Most of us were already familiar with at least some of Lowell's poetry, just as we had been with some of Stevens' and Williams'. But "Mr. Lowell," as Miss Bishop usually referred to him, was currently on the Harvard faculty. Some of us had had courses with him; all of us had met him, or, at least, heard him read his work. Miss Bishop had known him for nearly thirty years (they were introduced to each other by Randall Jarrell in 1946), and occasionally we would see them casually walking together near Harvard Square. Several of Lowell's poems were dedicated to her, and she had written the dust-jacket blurb for the first edition of *Life Studies,* reserved for us at the library. Now we were in Cambridge with her, reading Lowell's poems, living among the places and things he wrote about: the Boston Common, with Saint-Gaudens' monument to Colonel Shaw and his black regiment; the Charles River; the towns of Salem and Concord; Copley Square and Harvard University. All this gave Lowell's work a special immediacy. And if, twenty minutes or so into class, Miss Bishop slipped, as she sometimes did, and referred to "Mr. Lowell" as "Cal" we felt a thrill of complicity, as though she were sharing some secret with us.

Such slips were not common. She tried very hard to maintain a distance in discussing Lowell's poetry. While we students revelled in her occasional reminiscences, she sensed the incompatibility of talking about Lowell as a friend and trying to discuss his poetry objectively as a teacher. Consequently, Lowell was the only poet we studied about whom she did not spend a great deal of time filling us in with biographical information. Instead, she lavished odd bits of historical, literary, and geographical information on us as we read each poem. She was particularly thorough in explaining local references in Lowell's poetry. Whenever he mentioned a Boston neighborhood or landmark, she would immediately ask how many of us had been there. Anyone who had not was given a full description plus directions on how to get there. Being a transplanted Californian, I hardly knew Boston at all. Soon Miss Bishop had me spending my free afternoons tramping through the Common looking for Hooker's statue and searching out the swan boats in the Public Garden. And she was right in thinking that one could learn more about Lowell's poetry by spending an hour walking around the State House than by reading an article on *Lord Weary's Castle*. The author of *North & South, Questions of Travel,* and *Geography III* took local topography seriously.

What she commented most about in Lowell's *Life Studies* was his ability to turn a phrase that summoned up a time and place. In the opening poem of the "Life Studies" sequence, "My Last Afternoon with Uncle Devereux Winslow," she singled out certain phrases for special praise (my italics):

> That's how I threw cold water
> on my Mother and Father's
> *watery martini pipe dreams* at
>   Sunday dinner.

> . . . my Great Aunt Sarah
> was learning *Samson and Delilah.*
> She *thundered on the keyboard*

> *of her dummy piano,*
> with gauze curtains like a
> boudoir table . . .
>
> . . . Aunt Sarah, risen like the phoenix
> from her bed of *troublesome snacks*
> *and Tauchnitz classics.*

Lines like these would send her off on a flurry of memories and associations, and then she would speak of "Life Studies" as if it were *her* family album. Every poem seemed like some snapshot from her childhood. She made us realize that what was so extraordinary about these poems was not that they were confessional or technically innovative but, rather, that they re-created perfectly a small world that had passed away.

Occasionally, she spoke of her own family background, but always indirectly. She never mentioned people or events—only places and things. Once, she told us about a family heirloom she had inherited—a mediocre little landscape painted by a great uncle she never knew. It was only after owning it for some time, she claimed, that she suddenly recognized the place it depicted. Decades apart, both she and her uncle had seen and been struck by the same ordinary place—a "small backwater" in Nova Scotia. She transposed this incident into her "Poem," in *Geography III,* for her poetry almost always drew its inspiration directly from life.

When we reached the end of "Life Studies," we came to "Skunk Hour," which bears the dedication "For Elizabeth Bishop." I knew that Lowell had claimed it was partly modelled on her poem "The Armadillo," but I had always wondered if there was something else behind the dedication. (This was back in the dark ages before Ian Hamilton's biography of Lowell.) Had she figured personally in any of the episodes the poem describes? I waited for her comments—she always explained dedications to us. But this dedication she skipped over, so I decided to be bold and ask her.

"Oh, yes, it is dedicated to me, isn't it?" she said. "I really can't remember why. I'm sure he had a reason. I think it was because one summer when I was visiting him up in Castine—that's up in Maine—we heard some noises out in the back yard, and when we looked we saw a family of skunks going through the garbage. He must have remembered I was there that night."

This explanation was hardly the revelation I had hoped for, but I sat there and pretended to be satisfied. The class continued, and for once she took us firmly in hand and began a splendid reading of the poem with hardly a word or comment wasted. When she came to the sixth stanza, she talked about how cleverly Lowell worked a line from a song into the poem.

> A car radio bleats,
> "Love, O careless Love. . . . " I hear
> my ill-spirit sob in each blood cell . . .

"Do you mean that's a real song?" someone asked.

Miss Bishop responded instantly with a look of polite horror which meant that someone had asked a stupid question. "You don't all know this song?" she asked.

We all shook our heads, and so there in the Kirkland House basement, with the pipes clanking overhead, she sang it to us in a gentle pianissimo.

Kirkland was one of Harvard's handsome neo-Georgian "river houses," situated near the Charles. The four undergraduates in the class lived in other river houses, close by, but Miss Bishop and I came from the opposite direction. Our class was so small and informal that we all left together, and unless I slipped out quickly the moment it ended, politeness dictated that Miss Bishop and I walk back toward Harvard Yard together. And politeness was a virtue nurtured in her seminar. Descending into the basement of Kirkland House after the horn-honking, shoulder-banging tumult of Harvard Square, one stepped back into a slower, more gracious world, in which no relationship was ever rushed or small courtesy hurried by. The frayed trappings of our subterranean salon, where those heating pipes were the only gilding on the ceiling and a faint smell from the rusty furnace occasionally mingled with our teacher's discreet cologne, could make this gentility seem hardwon, but here for a few hours each week decorum triumphed over decor. Each of us was addressed as "Mr." or "Miss," even the mildest expletives were deleted, and gentlemen were expected to open doors for ladies.

Unstated rules of etiquette are often the most inflexible. By holding the door for our instructor during our exodus from the Kirkland underworld, I tacitly agreed to accompany her to Harvard Yard.

Likewise, I knew instinctively from the change in her voice as we
rose blinking into the sober light of day that all talk of poetry was now
expected to cease. At first, I thought that this sharp division between
her professional and her social identities was simply another example
of her unusual propriety. Not till much later did I realize how much
Miss Bishop dreaded all literary conversation. Under duress, she
might talk a little about poetry, but as soon as possible she would
change the subject.

She once told me a story that epitomized her attitude. Northrop
Frye, as the Norton Professor that year, was the guest of honor at a
dinner party one night to which Miss Bishop was invited. She was
embarrassed, she told me, because she hadn't read any of his books,
and then was horrified to discover that she had been seated next to
him at dinner. As the meal began, she leaned over to him and
confessed, "I've never read any of your books." "Wonderful!" Frye
replied, obviously relieved. They spent the rest of the evening chatting
about Nova Scotia.

My difficulty in talking with her on our first after-class jaunts
stemmed from the opposite problem. I had read all her books, and my
admiration intimidated me. At first, my shyness and her formality
provoked discussions mainly of a meteorological nature. Then, one
afternoon, for no apparent reason (though perhaps some fortunate
black cat crossed the path of my imagination), I mentioned that my
mother, back in Los Angeles, was trying to breed Himalayan kittens.
I was immediately besieged by detailed questions, and from that
moment we never lacked for lively conversation. Our favorite topics
were pets, flowers, fruit trees, church music, and travel, which usually
took me to California and her, inevitably, to Brazil, where, she
assured me, the orchids grew even on telephone lines. On rare
occasions, we even talked about books. Soon we began stopping
occasionally "for tea" at a nearby Russian restaurant, where we both
invariably drank coffee.

As the semester progressed, the undergraduates grew openly impa-
tient with Miss Bishop's singular ways. Their efforts at memorization
became so halfhearted and their recitations so halting and resentful
that in April this opprobrious requirement was quietly dropped. By
then, this capitulation scarcely mattered to the unhappy few. English
285 was not the course they had hoped for, and outside class some of

them had begun referring to it as "Studies in Elizabeth Bishop." One student, a bright, broad-shouldered member of the Crimson football squad, summed up their despair. "I could have taken Lowell's class," he groaned. "He's going to be in all the anthologies."

Morale was not helped by the long seminar paper due in late April. We were asked to choose any modern poet (except the three discussed in class) and write an introductory essay on his or her work. In class a few weeks before the papers were due, Miss Bishop asked us which poets we had selected. No one volunteered an immediate answer, but after further questioning she learned that none of the undergraduates had made up their minds and that I had chosen Georg Trakl, a modern Austrian poet, whose work was then almost unknown in America. After some discussion, she reluctantly agreed to my unorthodox topic but not before suggesting—politely, of course—that I had squeezed this foreigner into her course through a loophole. I knew then that I had better write a good paper. But my troubles had just begun. At the next session, all but one of the other students announced that they, too, were writing on foreign poets. Across the tiny table, I felt the cold heat of a long stare. It was the kind of look that directors call a "slow fuse"—a look like Oliver Hardy's glare the moment before he brains poor Stan Laurel and exclaims "Here's another fine mess you've gotten us into!" More merciful than Mr. Hardy, Miss Bishop let me off with only that stare, and, hopelessly outnumbered, acquiesced in our collective xenomania, but not before asking, "What's wrong with the English language?"

Ten days after I submitted my *opus magnum* on Trakl, I received an envelope from Miss Bishop containing my essay and a typed letter. Neither the letter nor the paper's title page bore a grade. Flipping through my essay, I saw that every page had dozens of corrections, queries, deletions, and suggestions in Miss Bishop's spidery hand. Some pages had obviously been worked over three times—once in blue ink, then in red, and, finally, in the proverbial blue pencil. In horror, I began reading marginal comments like "Awful expression," "Unnecessary phrase," "A mouthful," "Not in the dictionary"— most of which were followed by an exclamation point, as was her ubiquitous and incontrovertible "No!" An occasional "Better" or "Yes" (no exclamation point) did little to revive my self-confidence. I

had been weighed in the balance and found wanting. Only then did I
turn to the covering letter, which began:

Dear Mr. Gioia:
   You'll see that I have made many, many small marks and suggestions
on your paper, but this is really because it is very good, very well-
expressed, and I'd just like it to be even *better*-expressed, and, here and
there, to read more smoothly.

If this was indeed a "very good" paper, I wondered, what happened
to the bad ones? Then I noticed that even her own covering letter
bore half a dozen revisions. Looking back over my paper, I saw that
all but three of the hundreds of marks concerned questions of style.
Was there a better word? Was this phrase necessary? Was I using a
literary word when an everyday one would do? "When in doubt,"
she wrote at the bottom of one especially profound page, "use the
shorter word."
   By this time, I had realized that, for all her fumbling disorganiza-
tion, Miss Bishop had devised—or perhaps merely improvised—a
way of teaching poetry which was fundamentally different from the
manner conventionally professed in American universities. She never
articulated her philosophy in class, but she practiced it so consistently
that it is easy—especially now, a decade later—to see what she was
doing. She wanted us to see poems, not ideas. Poetry was the
particular way the world could be talked about only in verse, and
here, as one of her fellow-Canadians once said, the medium was the
message. One did not interpret poetry; one experienced it. Showing
us how to experience it clearly, intensely, and, above all, directly was
the substance of her teaching. One did not need a sophisticated
theory. One needed only intelligence, intuition, and a good dictionary.
There was no subtext, only the text. A painter among Platonists, she
preferred observation to analysis, and poem to poetry.
   Our final examination surprised even me. A take-home test, it ran a
full typed page (covered with the hand-scrawled corrections that by
now were her trademark) and posed us four tasks unlike any we had
ever seen on a college English exam. Furthermore, we were given
exact word lengths and citation requirements, as well as this admoni-

tion as a headline: "Use only your books of poems and a dictionary; please do not consult each other."

First, the final asked us to "find, and write out, for each of our three poets, two examples of: simile, metaphor, metonymy, oxymoron, synesthesia." That seemed odd but easy. Second, we were asked to reread Williams' "The Descent" and answer a number of questions about what particular phrases meant as well as to find parallel passages in Lowell and Stevens. Third, we were asked to "paraphrase Lowell's 'Skunk Hour' as simply as possible, first giving the *story,* what is happening in each stanza: who, when, where," and then to answer a battery of questions about particular persons, places, times, and phrases in the poem. "Be brief!" Miss Bishop had scrawled at the end of her two paragraphs of instructions for this question. These questions were unusual but not altogether unexpected, since they reflected her classroom method. It was Question No. 4 that left everyone at a loss:

> Now please try your hand at 24 lines of original verse; three poems of eight lines each, in imitation of the three poets studied, in their styles and typical of them. (In the case of Lowell, the style of *Lord Weary's Castle.*) I don't expect these pastiches to be great poetry!—but try to imitate (or parody if you prefer) the characteristic subject-matter, meter, imagery, and rhyme (if appropriate).

We may not have consulted each other about the answers to this test, but, walking out of Kirkland after the last class with the final in our hands, we could not help talking about the questions. Miss Bishop had gone off to her office, and we were alone.

"I can't believe it," one of the undergraduates moaned. "We have to write poems."

Someone else offered the consolation that at least everything else on the exam was easy.

"Yeah, but we still have to write poems."

Later that week, turning in my final exam at Miss Bishop's office, I stopped to visit her one last time before I left for California. A student's farewell to a favorite teacher is usually a sombre ritual, and I approached this occasion with the requisite melancholy. Entering her office, I wondered if I would ever see her again.

She seemed glad to see me. Indeed, she appeared generally more cheerful and carefree than I had seen her in weeks. She launched immediately into uncharacteristically lighthearted chatter, against which my youthful solemnity proved an inadequate defense. We talked for almost an hour. She even asked for my California address—that meant there would be letters. I enjoyed the visit but was slightly puzzled nonetheless. I had never seen her so animated. It was only as I rose to leave that I understood. More than any of her students, she was overjoyed that classes were over.

Index

"Abou Ben Adhem," 4
Academic Center of the School of Minas, Ouro Prêto, 47–48
Adams, Léonie, 7, 28, 44–45
Alfred, William, 139
Amazon River, 30, 115, 116
Amazonas, Brazil, 51, 75, 78
American School, Rio de Janeiro, 113
Ames, Elizabeth, 131
Andersen, Hans Christian, 20
Andrade, Carlos Drummond de, 10, 16, 49, 52, 53, 79, 85, 96; "Travelling in the Family," 85
Andrade, Mario de, 19
Anglo-Catholicism, 129
Anhambi, 9
Anjinhos, 120
Antarctic, 60
Apollinaire, Guillaume, 40
Araújo, Lili Corrêa de, 47, 48, 96
Arctic, 60
Argentina, 47, 52
Aristophanes, 10
Aristotle, 123
Arkansas, 122, 135
Armstrong, Phyllis, 131
Aruba, 88
Ashbery, John, 60, 74, 140–41; "Self-Portrait in a Convex Mirror," 140
Assis, Machado de, 10
Astaire, Fred, 115
Auden, Wystan H., 23, 24, 34, 44, 66, 88, 90, 103, 112, 128, 141; *Collected Poems,* 138; *Journal to a War,* 66; "On the Frontier," 88

Babylon (Babilonia), Rio de Janeiro, 15, 29
Bahia, Brazil, 78
Baker, Howard, 23
Baldwin, James, 15
Bandeira, Manuel, 10, 75, 77, 79
Baudelaire, Charles, 18, 37
Beats, 34–35
Belitt, Ben, 109
Bell, Alexander Graham, 82

Belle Isle, Newfoundland, 83
Belo Horizonte, Minas Gerais, 48, 124
Bennington College, 109
Bernardes, Sérgio, 14
Berryman, John, 52, 96
Best Short Stories of 1948, 7
Bible, the, 10
Bidart, Frank, 119
Bishop, Elizabeth: **Awards, Prizes:** Academy of American Poets Fellowship (American Academy of Poets Award), 14, 54, 56, 74, 98; American Academy of Arts and Letters, 69, 105; American Institute of Arts and Letters, 9; Amy Lowell Fellowship, 56; Books Abroad/Neustadt International Prize for Literature, 57–58, 59, 74, 98, 105; Consultant in Poetry at the Library of Congress, 3, 9, 28, 31, 56, 131; Guggenheim Fellowship, 6, 9, 14, 54, 56, 117; Houghton Mifflin Fellowship in Poetry, 9, 31, 56, 60; Ingram-Merrill Foundation Grant, 74; Lucy Martin Donnelly Fellowship, Bryn Mawr College, 9; National Book Award, 33, 50, 51, 56, 59, 69, 72, 74, 98, 105; National Book Critics Circle, 69, 72, 73, 105; Order of Rio Branco (Order of the Baron of Rio Branco), 56, 74; Partisan Review Fellowship in Poetry, 9, 14; Pulitzer Prize, 8, 9, 14, 30, 33, 48, 50, 51, 54, 56, 57, 59, 69, 70, 74, 78, 98, 105, 124–25; Rockefeller Foundation Grant, 53; Shelley Memorial Award, 9, 54, 56
Brazil: allergy and illness in, 14, 31, 52, 70, 74; American interest in, 16; "anjinhos," Bishop's shadow box, 120; arrival and stay in, 8, 18; artists in, 49; car in, 119; "Black Beans and Diamonds," unwritten book about, 29; Casa Mariana in, 31; cats in, 9, 18, 80; descriptions of, 8–9, 152; French influence in, 19, 79; grocer with lucky customers in, 56, 70, 78, 125; influence of, in Bishop's life, 18–19; mail in, 50, 121; racial democracy in, 16; scenery in, 17; temperament in, 75–76; theories about, 80; thinking in, 79; trip up Rio São Francisco in, 115; way of life in, 16–17